THE
REAGAN
YEARS

THE REAGAN YEARS

Hodding Carter

GEORGE BRAZILLER / NEW YORK

The articles that appear in this book have been published as they originally appeared in *The Wall Street Journal.*

Published in the United States in 1988
by George Braziller, Inc.

For information address the publisher:

George Braziller, Inc.
60 Madison Avenue
New York, New York 10010

Designed by Lesley Blakeney

Library of Congress Cataloging-in-Publication Data
Carter, Hodding.
The Reagan years.
Bibliography: p.
1. United States—Politics and government—1981- 1.
2. Reagan, Ronald. I. Title.
E876.C377 1988 973.927 88-16729
ISBN 0-8076-1209-X

First Printing, September 1988

To Betty Werlein Carter—A Mighty Force

CONTENTS

PART TWO: THE FOREIGN SCENE

INTRODUCTION

Ronald Reagan owned the first eight years of the 1980s. He set the national agenda, defined most of the terms of the national dialogue, and dominated what passed for national political debate. For a reputedly passive man, he had a more pervasive impact on the country than anyone since Franklin D. Roosevelt.

Looking back over these chronologically and thematically arranged columns written for the *Wall Street Journal* between late 1980 and mid-1988, it isn't surprising to discover that Ronald Reagan was at the center of most of them. I would have been happier if it had been otherwise. An openly partisan liberal Democrat for most of my life, from early teens to current middle age, I was appalled by the voters' decisions in 1980 and 1984 and even more appalled by most of the president's domestic and foreign policies.

On the other hand, I was pleasantly surprised when the *Journal* decided to inaugurate an op-ed experiment, just as the Reagan era was beginning, with me as one of the contributors to its Thursday edition liberal ghetto. If you are going to suffer, it's nice to have a towering platform from which to bellow your rage and sorrow.

The op-ed section of most newspapers is ordinarily the page facing the editorial page—thus, opposite (op) editorial (ed). It is the tiny homage offered by the quasi-monopolists of the daily press to elementary notions of balance and diversity.

For those who run the *Journal*'s editorial section, however, the op-ed venture was no casual gesture. The newspaper's editor, Robert L. Bartley, takes more seriously than all but a handful of other American journalists his right to provide vigorous, unfettered and unrestrained views on a wide range of subjects. As seen from his perch far on the political right, those who disagree on the basics are not merely wrong, but are also variously idiotic, incompetent, dangerous, or semi-subversive.

His is a standard of editorial clarity that I respect with roughly the same intensity that I reject most of his positions. It seemed only logical and fair, therefore, to try to bring the same vigor to my assessment of the Reagan years that the Bartley brigade brought to theirs. In this context, "fair" might not be the word our adversaries would apply to either approach, but so be it. Mush is the enemy of reason.

Sharp opinions openly offered came naturally to me by 1980. From 1959, when I came home after a two-year hitch with the Marines, until early 1977, when I joined the Carter administration for a three-and-a-half year tour as State Department spokesman, I was the chief editorial voice of the *Delta Democrat-Times,* our family-owned daily in Greenville, Mississippi. Those were the years of racial revolution in the South and of near-revolutionary adjustments of attitude and behavior for many whites, including me. My father, who with my mother, founded the newspaper in 1936 to take on an entrenched monopoly, was what was then called a "Southern moderate." He was a brave man who wrestled all his life with the conflict between his segregationist heritage and the manifest demands of his religious and political faith. Dad won, which meant the moral imperatives increasingly prevailed in what he wrote for a national as well as a local audience. When it came time for me to face the conflict, that made it easier for me than it had been for him, and easier, too, than it was for many of my Southern contemporaries.

Not that it was ever easy, for Dad, for me, or for most other Southerners who chose to dissent, white or black. It was a wrenching experience, frightening at times and, in ways large and small, occasionally costly. White supremacy exacted conformity as a necessary concomitant, and militant segregationists were prepared to enforce it with economic intimidation and physical violence. Except in rare instances, the latter was reserved for blacks, but the threat always hovered in the background.

That is probably of only marginal interest to anyone who didn't live through it. The South has changed dramatically, its racial practices and problems today little different from the nation's as a whole. But the experience of those years helps explain how and why I believe government should play a role. During that violent period, the federal government with mounting energy forced an openly repressive, openly undemocratic society to abandon *de jure* segregation, its most cherished institution. It was the federal government, first through the courts and then through Congress and the White House, which offered hope and then implementation of far-reaching change. Without federal law and pressure, the South would still be mired in its centuries-old infatuation with what was routinely referred to as "our way of life." Before they were brought into play, the rate of change was glacial. The resistance to change was massive.

You'll read variations on that theme later in this book. But it was not just in matters of race that my environment shaped my view of the proper role of government. My native region was a microcosm of explanation and justification for activist central government.

From highways to waterways, only Washington could provide the central planning, financing and direction necessary to build the transportation system without which our economically backward state could not develop. It was Washington that finally legislated a comprehensive substitute for the prevailing devil-take-the-hindmost system of local flood-control districts. Federal funds provided agricultural research and information to cope with insects and plant disease. Federal legislation created hospitals where there had been none, housing for those who grown up in primitive hovels, a college education for men and women whose parents had been lucky to go to grammar school.

"The government is the problem," Ronald Reagan is still fond of saying, eight years after he was elected to lead the government. In my Mississippi and all the urban and rural counterparts to Mississippi across the land, the existence of poverty, ignorance, racism, and inadequate housing were the problems. Government was the solution.

Just as that was not the view of Ronald Reagan and millions of other Americans in the 1980s, it was not the view of those who ruled Mississippi thirty years ago. But the Mississippi experience speaks to the national in this respect as well. None were more forceful advocates of government action to save the local economy than the planters and bankers of the Mississippi Delta in the 1930s. None more rapidly resumed their opposition to big government than those same leaders once their particular crises had receded and the programs that benefitted them were securely in place.

In a not dissimilar way, government became the "problem" for millions of middle-class Americans only after their entitlements, once considered wildly radical innovations, were lodged in political concrete. Then an old joke once beloved of liberal Democrats returned to haunt them with a new spin. "Thank God for the

Democratic party," went the punch line. "It made it possible for me to live like a Republican." Next, to think like one as well.

That is not necessarily a bad thing. Fairness and a slight sense of history compel me to admit that long-term political hegemony by any party is, at a minimum, conducive to corruption. At worst, it is destructive of democratic government. As it is, the Democratic party has yet to reinvigorate itself after its long run as the only show in town. The party, in fact, contradicts several laws of physics. While nature abhors a vacuum, the Democratic party exists with one at its core. Around that intellectual and conceptual void revolves an entire solar system of competing planets held in inexplicable orbit.

Well, perhaps not completely inexplicable. There is actually a force of sorts at the center of those loose constellations. It is the lust for power. What should be done with power once attained is not something about which Democrats agree or on which they are inclined to dwell overlong. When they do, their sharp cleavages threaten to break the mystical power-bond that holds them within the same framework.

The nation's oldest political organization is less a party than a loose confederation of liberals, a few stray radicals, neo-everythings, and a host of practicing politicians concerned about the next election. When faced by a competing power center with a clear purpose and a leader with clearly stated, consistent ideas, such as the Republican party presented in the early 1980s, it is reduced to a pitiful puddle of incoherence and a bad case of policy stutters.

Past success and past failure are equally culpable. The success was Lyndon Johnson's completion of the New Deal wish list. Virtually all of the old, unfinished business was wrapped up in one legislative package or another. Capitalizing on an explosively expansive economy, the Great Society admitted to few limits. In a burst of extraordinary legislative energy, roadblocks to civil rights, educational opportunity, society welfare, and adequate housing were obliterated. The Democratic party's consensus was legislatively formalized as the American consensus.

Behind that accomplishment marched legions of competing interests for which no consensus existed. New rights were claimed, new entitlements demanded, new causes advanced about which there was deep division, nowhere more evident than within the party itself. Where its leaders were not divided, they were almost literally exhausted. The 1960s were traumatic for many Americans; they were debilitating for the Democrats, not least because they drew down the last of their capital from the bank.

The party's spasm of completion and depletion occurred at roughly the same time that the national foreign policy consensus was also disintegrating. Party activists knew what they were passionately against. The party was unable to formulate what it stood for. Vietnam was the Democrats' war; the Democratic party became its most notable noncombatant casualty. There was irony aplenty that the creators of anticommunist internationalism in the late 1940s splintered over its disastrous misapplication in the 1960s.

That was the background for the rise of Ronald Reagan and the Republican right. Their triumph is an impressive story and an encouraging one for anyone who labors in the political wilderness. It is a textbook case of will and conviction overcoming ridicule and failure.

"I think I can," chugged the one-time, second-tier movie actor as he carried the right-wing gospel around a Great Society nation after the Goldwater slaughter of 1964. "I think I can," he said as he surprised everyone by being elected governor of California over an experienced, popular Democratic politician. "I think I can," he repeated, despite rejections of his presidential aspirations by the GOP in 1968 and 1976. "I think I can," he echoed as columnists and commentators denigrated his message and his prospects in the long run-up to November 1980. "I did it," he finally could proclaim, having crushed first a sitting President and then the perfect exemplar of the Democratic party's soul in 1984.

Critics to the contrary, the president's was not a triumph of style over substance, but of persuasive substance given voice by a masterful communicator. What he promised was straightforward and simple. The United States would regain military supremacy over the Soviet Union, a supremacy it had allegedly lost in the 1970s and whose loss seriously threatened its very survival. He would reinvigorate a faltering economy by taking government off the necks of business and industry, by cutting taxes and slashing welfare waste, fraud, and abuse. Under his leadership, the United States would stop kicking itself around and would instead concentrate on the positive. We were the last, best hope of mankind, and it was time we were saying it again. Any enemy of our enemy was our friend, and an undue concern about human rights was yesterday's trivial pursuit.

Ronald Reagan also triumphed with a major assist from his opposition's failure in office. A president who campaigned against a background of double-digit inflation, eight million unemployed and twenty percent interest rates was in trouble. A president simultaneously saddled with the dilemma posed by Americans held hostage in Teheran was twice cursed. Jimmy Carter's impotence was a daily reminder of the undigested humiliation of the Vietnam war. A challenger could not ask for much more than that, but Ronald Reagan got it anyway. He was also offered the gift of an opponent whose public style was as stilted as Reagan's was smooth.

Which brings us to the Reagan years, the focus of the columns that follow. Assessing the period is not as easy as the president's campaign rhetoric and themes suggested it might be in 1980. My advice to the contrary, he did not stay the course on everything he undertook. He occasionally made startling shifts in direction, proving on several occasions that the most ideological president in American history could rise above principle and do the right thing.

That was most notably true in the president's evolving response to the challenge (and opportunity) provided by Mikhail Gorbachev's dramatic alteration of Soviet policies at home and abroad. In his first two years Mr. Reagan had offered arms reduction proposals, which were clearly meant to be rejected by a standpat Moscow, as they were. But when Gorbachev pivoted the Soviet response on a dime and said yes, first to a total elimination of intermediate range missiles in Europe and then to deep cuts in strategic weapons, the president swiveled just as adroitly. He sent his right-wing advisers and hard-core supporters into manic depression by going forward with the first deal and pushing hard for the second. No matter that neither would have been possible without Gorbachev. What did matter was that Ronald Reagan shook hands with the leader of the "evil empire" and thereby shook up East-West relations as they had not been shaken since the advent of the Cold War forty years earlier.

Ronald Reagan was also president during a period of sustained economic growth—the Reagan boom—following the most severe economic shakeout since the Great Depression—the Reagan bust. Again, no matter that credit for much of this success had to do with factors over which he had no control, such as Federal

Reserve Chairman Paul Volcker's tenacity and the collapse of commodity prices. Nor did anyone except partisan debaters care that the recovery proceeded in ways and from causes undreamed of by the prophets of the supply-side gospel. Roaring consumer demand and the pump priming of soaring federal deficits were the fuel, Keynesian staples both. On the other hand, little that the supply-siders and the president so confidently predicted in the way of specifics came to pass. The budget was never brought close to balance, in theory or reality. Personal savings rates shrank rather than grew. New plant and equipment investment played a negligible role in the first phases of the recovery. And to the surprise of everyone, the Fed's high interest rates clubbed inflation to the floor.

But who really cared about keeping that kind of score? What counted were the results. By the end of the Reagan era, new jobs were being created almost as rapidly as during the 1970s. Inflation was under the tightest control since the 1960s, while unemployment had moved from a forty-year high to a fourteen-year low. These were all unalloyed successes; they happened during the Reagan years and he deserved credit, if not all the credit, for them.

There was success on another front as well. Shortly before Mr. Reagan took office, I gave him some gratuitous advice. Ignore the establishment's conventional wisdom and act decisively to produce what you promised in the campaign. He didn't need the advice. He and his team moved with brilliant tactical skill to ram his tax cut and budget reduction program through Congress early in his first term. Those Democrats who didn't roll over were rolled, while the Republicans voted as a monolithic bloc. On a related front, the president later stole tax reform as an issue and never totally relinquished it. History is likely to give the administration a lion's share of the credit for that fundamental reshaping of fiscal policy, whatever history's verdict on the merits.

Ideological mulishness delayed, but did not finally prevent, the advent of sound judgment about the dollar. Free markets at home and abroad were a talisman of Reaganite faith, and a strong dollar was supposed to be proof of the faith's validity. As a result, the president cheered on the appreciation of the dollar to heights that eliminated American products from foreign markets while indirectly subsidizing foreign competition at home. The trade figures took off in the wrong direction and the trade deficit reached unprecedented levels.

Rigidity could not withstand the test of common sense. The administration's resident pragmatist, Treasury Secretary James Baker, maneuvered a total reversal of the old policy. The dollar went into something akin to free-fall, American manufactured goods became more price-competitive, and the trade deficit began to shrink.

So much for the good news about the Reagan years, unless the military victory of a nation of 240 million citizens over an island-state of 125 thousand is considered noteworthy. That short burst of gunboat diplomacy coincided almost exactly with the bloody debacle at the Marine barracks in Beirut, a bracketing which provides the necessary perspective for judging both.

On the home front, the Reagan years were not benign, though Ronald Reagan's public persona is unfailingly warm and benign. The administration's domestic policies seemed to rest squarely on the proposition that government should comfort the comfortable and afflict the afflicted, if only by shortchanging or ignoring them. The rich got richer, the poor got poorer, and the middle class improved its lot by sending more family members into the marketplace and having fewer children. Essential public services in areas such as child care, housing, and education were savagely slashed or frozen.

Black America ceased to exist as a meaningful factor in federal calculations, except in ways detrimental to blacks. The president's Justice Department spent the eight years trying to find ways to reverse longstanding civil rights policies. Extension of the Voting Rights Act in effective form had to be forced on a reluctant White House. Congress and the courts kept the President from providing tax exemption as a reward for segregation academies' racist admission policies. The Justice Department's assault on affirmative action was unremitting. The perversion of the Civil Rights Commission's mission by the Reagan appointees led to its virtual demise, perhaps according to a hidden script.

When and where the administration was unable to convince Congress that federal regulations were too onerous to bear, foxes were placed in the regulatory henhouses as well. Some caused scandal, as at the Environmental Protection Agency in the early 1980s. Some did everything they could to subvert the spirit of the law, as at the Federal Trade Commission. Many were so enthused by the doctrine that government is the enemy of the public good that their behavior made a compelling argument for their case. Fortunately for the long-term health of the nation, most Americans rejected the particulars of the Reagan antigovernment manifesto, and that rejection stiffened Congress's spine.

Wretched is the only word to use for the petty thieves, moral midgets, and grand poltroons who pockmarked the administration from beginning to end. The sheer numbers are damning. Indictments, convictions, forced resignations, slippery evasions, and a general contempt for the rule of law were hallmarks of the Reagan years. Not since Warren Harding had so many federal officials so thoroughly ignored the admonition that public service is a public trust. The successive crises of Edwin Meese at the White House and Justice Department were illustrative.

More disturbing than moral myopia was the true-believing certitude that underlay the adventures of the security state warriors who perched at the National Security Council, the CIA, and the State Department. So confident were they of the righteousness of their cause that they trafficked with terrorists and drug dealers, made war without authorization, and conducted secret operations "off the shelf" and out of control. The Constitution was a trifle, accountability began and ended with deniability, and Congress was an anachronistic barrier to the salvation of the free world. Their ventures were uniformly as disastrous as they were harebrained, embarrassing to the administration and to the nation. Aside from the body-count carnage underwritten by their secret war games, the most serious damage caused by the comic book cowboys was to the fragile fabric of responsive, representative government.

At the root of Iran-Contra and its many clones was the hard right's conviction that we live in a Manichean world. The United States is absolute good. The Soviet Union represents absolute evil. Every conflict, every problem, every confrontation, and every disagreement is ultimately definable by reference to the struggle with Moscow. Because the Soviets are evil and we are not, whatever we or our friends do to counter them is, ipso facto, good. Thus when our "freedom fighter" clients blow up a school bus in Nicaragua, it is a just act in a just war. When our adversaries do something similar, they are terrorists.

The president managed by the end of his term to have it both ways without going visibly crazy. He fronted for a policy in Central America based squarely on the light-dark division of the world, while dealing with the heart of darkness on a matter-of-fact basis. It was far more than his ideological soul mates could manage or swallow.

If Ronald Reagan was able to discern basic changes in Soviet attitudes, as he seemed to say several times in 1988, he never deviated one iota from the conviction that massive military spending was a once and future necessity for America. He came into office vowing to close the so-called window of vulnerability. He came to the end of his second term with that window, as defined by his defense strategists in 1981, still wide open. In between, he spent some two trillion dollars on a military buildup that armor-plated the economy, gold-plated the country's weapon systems, underwrote a pie-in-the-sky bid for total strategic defense in space—and made no appreciable difference in the military balance.

That was not because the Russians spent vast amounts as well. It was because the assertion that the Soviet Union had "surged ahead" was always a fraud, in large part because it rested on the premise that nuclear war was "winnable." If it were not, then sufficiency for deterrence was enough, and American sufficiency was never in serious doubt. Indeed, as the Reagan era wound down, Soviet revelations about their defense capacity combined with American reassessment of previous analyses of Soviet spending combined to produce a picture of long-term parity rather than imbalance.

The military spending binge did have one measurable effect that made a sizeable difference, and it was damaging to national security. The president's refusal to pay for the buildup was the proximate cause for the doubling (and more) of the national debt during the Reagan years. His certainty that defense spending was the most significant index of national strength blinded him to the primacy of economic factors. Japan and other onrushing competitors loved the Reagan fixation. As Jesse Jackson was fond of observing, there was a ready market for their VCRs; where was the market for our MX?

For a nation supposedly dominated by the power of the mass media, the 1980s were not vintage years for the press. It is difficult to find the facts to support the popular delusion that the media set the national agenda. For all of the first term and at least the first half of the second, the hand on the media spotlight was invariably the administration's. When it said that terrorism rather than human rights was the focus of foreign policy, terrorism became a journalistic obsession. When it said that Central America would be the determinative battleground in the East-West struggle, the cameras and reporters discovered Central America. When it wanted to keep tax cuts and budget reductions at center stage, they stayed there. And whenever it announced that something new was now all-consuming, whether the Middle East or arms talks or drugs, the focus dutifully changed.

The fact is that the most damaging controversies involving the president and his policies were not developed or initiated by the media. They were either accidental gifts in the form of circumstance, or outright gifts as with the Iran-Contra scandal. Had it not been for a Beirut magazine, an Iranian politician, and Attorney General Meese, we might still know nothing of the sale of arms to Iran and the diversion of the proceeds to the Contras.

Former administration officials volunteered information in their deluge of kiss-and-tell books that eluded most of the press throughout the Reagan years. David Stockman blew the whistle on the administration's funny-money budget building. Alexander Haig's depiction of the foreign-policy-making and implementation process was hair-curling, an early warning which received too little serious attention. Donald Regan's book, astrology aside, filled in a portrait of a president who knew what he wanted in the broadest terms, but had only a tenuous grasp of what it might mean or cost.

The costs face post-Reagan America. The word "staggering" when applied to the massive increase in the national debt is now a cliché, but is no less appropriate for being overused. The structural deficit is a reality, not a rationalization, and neither party seems inclined to face up to its consequences. The nation clearly does not grasp all the implications of being the world's most prodigious debtor. Foreigners will soon hold a trillion dollars of U.S. IOUs. They will want something more for their money than political abuse from the drunken sailors who signed them.

So, too, the steady stratification of a have and have-not society must either be soon reversed, at high cost, or allowed to proceed at even higher cost. The latter will be charged against the nature of our society as well as the public treasury. Abraham Lincoln had it right. We could not endure half-slave and half-free, and we cannot endure as we are, two-thirds the beneficiaries of the American promise, one-third frozen out. At least, we cannot endure and still be the America of our aspirations and promise.

At root, what was wrong with the Reagan years and the president's political philosophy was that they minimized community in favor of individual aggrandizement. They stressed the efficacy of military force in a world in which it has only limited utility as an effective instrument of national policy. They justified brutal behavior abroad and illegal activity at home by placing ends over means. And they turned their backs on the real meaning of this "shining city set on the hill," as cited by the president in his first inaugural address. What glitters there is not gold, but a principle, one enunciated centuries ago: "For of those to whom much is given, much is required."

That is what I hope I was saying in these columns over the last eight years. See if you agree.

Part One

THE DOMESTIC SCENE

1

The Administration and the Media

November 1, 1981

Once upon a time there was a man who lived in a big white house. He was not the first man to live in it by a long shot, and with any luck at all he wouldn't be the last, but he was the one living there now.

The man, who had a grand job with many responsibilities and dependents, had a staff of commensurate size. Each person on it had a function, and some had multiple functions, but no function was more important than the task of those who managed the kennel.

As kennels go, it was not particularly magnificent or imposing, but almost all the dogs of the land looked upon it as canine Valhalla, particularly the younger dogs. They felt that the master of the house needed them almost as much as they needed him, and they also knew that if he fed them well, they would prosper and loom ever larger in dogdom.

Many of them had spent years as hunting dogs, roaming and foraging on their own in far-flung woods. Most were accustomed to being nurtured by many sources rather than one, so that their first months in the big white house were occasionally frustrating. At feeding time, few were the hands carrying the meat and much was the meat without real substance.

But when the choice pieces were placed before them, glorious was the feast and envious were their peers in less well-stocked quarters.

Indeed, the spectacle of their gnawing over the meal so carefully prepared for their taste was the subject of much attention throughout the land. It reflected well on the house and its residents as well.

But some asked why those in the great white house would care about such things. Would it not be sufficient simply to provide plain, nourishing meals for the kennel dogs at regular intervals, saving the best for very special occasions when there was something significant to celebrate? For that matter, was it not the nature of dogs to provide for themselves? Should they not be turned loose to scare up rabbits and run down an occasional deer?

Such questions betrayed a basic misunderstanding of the reason the man in the white house had the dogs close at hand. The last thing he wanted was for them to follow their basic instincts. Feeding and stroking and gentling insured that they would perform as required, rather than behave like normal dogs, which occasionally bite the hand that feeds them.

No, it was well known that if the master and his staff deviated from what the dogs had come to see as their right, if those who ran the white house said to the dogs, "You are dogs and we are people and we have different roles and different functions and different responsibilities, so you get about your business while we stick to ours," the dogs might do almost anything.

Some might bark loudly, disturbing the neighbors. Some might begin coursing through the white house halls, sniffing out the many different meals behind closed doors. Others might so forget themselves as to turn upon the master and his minions, rending and tearing and raising general hell, forgetting that dog, staff and master were and should be a symbiotic team, playing to and for the same outside world.

Such had happened before, much to the distress of the men who lived in the white house. Some of the staff had worked in the house in those days as well, and they knew what the dogs could do if things went badly, particularly if cheered on and encouraged by an audience beyond the high fence. While no one currently seemed particularly interested in such a spectacle, they knew that dogs will be dogs if you aren't careful, and an ounce of prevention is worth a pound of cure, as their mothers used to say.

No one understood this better than the lord of the manor. He had been dealing with dogs, in good days and bad, for what seemed like generations. He had learned what could make a dog crawl on its belly and wag its tail, and what could bring a dog to bristling alert, searching for an opening to the jugular. Through it all, as staff and kennel dogs alike were happy to tell anyone who asked, he had come genuinely to like most dogs, and he showed it in many ways, like rubbing favored ones behind the ears and scratching their stomachs when they rolled over. (At such times, the dogs took on an uncanny resemblance to pussy cats.)

He was, in short, the model of a model white house occupant as far as many of the dogs were concerned, and they responded accordingly. Few barked and even fewer went hunting for game in the halls. When they did bark, it was usually at a time when the staff felt the barking was appropriate or helpful to the healthy functioning of the house. The dogs agreed among themselves that it was good to see a smooth routine reestablished in the kennel, with smiles and good food all around and a general sense of style that befitted the relationship.

And that was the image the dogs' behavior transmitted across the land: a well-ordered house, a well-stocked larder and a master who knew what he was doing. If most of the doors in the house remained closed, if some envious malcontents beyond the fence complained that there was more to the master's stewardship of the house than a good relationship with the dogs, few were those who paid much heed. The dogs were quiet, weren't they? And if they were quiet, all was well.

January 20, 1983

This is not going to be a column about presidential petulance when press relations go sour. That one was written about 10 months ago, at the time the president was going through the predictable White House exercise of blaming bad times on the reporters who detail its existence. You remember the period, when Mr. Reagan was annoyed by those 90-second accounts of the hard life of unemployed workers and their families in "South Succotash."

Instead, this seems an appropriate time to come at the same subject from a different angle. Appearances to the contrary, this and other administrations of the modern era are not engaged in total war with the Washington press corps, but instead both exist in a tightly symbiotic relationship that serves everyone's interests but those of the general public.

Putting it another way, they're engaged in a game in which only the players know the rules, in which most of the moves are baffling to the paying customers and in which the players' appreciation of each other's style and performance matter far more than the audience's.

Consider the rules of engagement. There are elaborate codes of conduct in which some material, almost always bland, is put on the record and attributed to visible human beings, while much of the most significant information is transmitted by unseen faces to print and broadcast outlets. This kind of information is given on background, or deep background, or off the record, etc., etc., and it provides the core of Washington political reporting.

It allows that well-known unknown, the "informed source" or "high administration official," to get his knife into an opponent or float a trial balloon without political danger. It permits a reporter to write a story which proves he is in the know, but protects him from the consequences of error, since he is simply relaying what the person behind the mask has said. And it provides useful reading for all the other participants in the Washington game, since they usually know enough to be able to make out, at least hazily, the identity of the source and the meaning of the message.

The problem is that the average reader or viewer can't do the same. The cascade of stories from one "White House aide" after another, flatly contradicting on consecutive days what other "White House aides" have said about the budget or the nuclear arms talks or whatever, thoroughly confuses most people. They know it is being reported in English, they think they have a program guide, but what they see is contradictory nonsense masquerading as information. It is not surprising that so many Americans simply turn off the set, put down the paper and take up other pastimes.

And the truth is, occasional flashes of presidential anger aside, this is really the way that policy makers and policy opponents want it. It provides "deniability," it allows a great deal of shooting from ambush and it insulates them from that most dread demand of all, accountability.

But why do reporters play by these rules with such vim and enthusiasm? Strip away the pious protestations that they could not provide adequate information to the rest of us if they did not engage in their elaborate minuet, and the explanation becomes a trifle sordid. If they are locked in so tight an embrace with the high and mighty, then they become high and mighty by association. No longer the lowly purveyors of facts and figures, of context and continuity, they can masquerade as "the fourth branch of government," the fourth estate, tribunes of the people.

From time to time, the public is given a look at what the world would be like if Washington reporters didn't play by the rules, when the veil is stripped away and real faces with real identities are tied to the news of the day. William Greider writes a long piece in the Atlantic, based on months of private conversations with budget director David Stockman, and provides more coherent insight into the ways of the Reagan presidency than 300 examples of the usual Washington journalism combined. More than a year-and-a-half after it would have done the public some real good, New York Times White House correspondent Steven Weisman writes a detailed account for the Times magazine of the early doubts of the president's chief advisers about the wisdom of his three-year tax program, naming names meticulously.

Back comes the standard reply to such criticism. "Everyone" knew all about it. It was all there in our stories at the time. Anyone who bothered to read what we wrote or watch what we put on the air would have known of Mr. Stockman's reservations and the various advisers' fears. Out come the clips and the stand-ups, and sure enough, there is some "White House source" saying exactly what we know Dave Stockman or Jim Baker or Murray Weidenbaum was saying.

Except that only the insiders could hope to identify the sources at the time. For the rest of America, it might as well have been in Greek. Warnings from within the temple of mysteries are not the same as warnings from flesh and blood people. But it is satisfying to be within the temple, interpreting the oracles while knowing there is more to the story than their utterances. Being a keeper of the mysteries inflates the ego far more than being an observer from outside. And so the game goes on in Washington, with no permanent loser except the people.

March 17, 1983

When it comes to having it up to your keister with the question of leaks, the average federal employee could give instruction to the president seven days a week and still have plenty of material left over. This administration's top officials regularly shoot themselves and their leader in the foot from ambush, then just as regularly try to handle the ensuing uproar by adopting new restrictions which suggest the problem is to be found in the bowels of the bureaucracy. In the process, they and the president assault common sense and the Constitution as well.

To belabor the record a little, it didn't seem possible that the White House could top the asininity of its proposed guidelines of January 1982, under which National Security Adviser William P. Clark recommended stringent restrictions on the way government employees should deal with the "national media" when the topic was foreign affairs and national security. The press loudly protested, cooler heads prevailed and the more objectionable portions of the proposed order were dropped.

But the fury about leaks which lay behind the abortive crackdown surfaced during the same period, when the Washington Post ran details of a secret session of the Defense Resources Board. At the meeting, military leaders were told that the administration's proposed five-year, $1.5 trillion defense program could cost up to 50% more than expected.

When that story broke, the hunt was on, with Defense Department officials using lie detectors right and left. For a while, it appeared they might actually have found their man, the director of manpower management in the office of the assistant secretary of defense for manpower. He denied it, the reporter who wrote the story stoutly denied the person was his source and eventually the matter faded.

In late 1982 and January of this year [1983], the White House staff was busily engaged in open war by leak to influence the president's budget decisions. The last straw was the New York

Times quote of a White House official who termed the budget process an "unmitigated disaster." Up came the president's keister and down came a new edict.

Henceforth, under new "Guidelines for Press Coordination," White House communications director David Gergen would clear all press interviews in advance or "designate" a White House official as the person to answer questions on a particular subject. "I would not call it a gag order," Gergen said. "We are going to try and serve you to insure that we get a full and free flow of information."

We all know how well that worked. Indeed, the man known to be one of the more adroit leakers at the White House, Chief of Staff James A. Baker III, was caught just a little earlier calling for Ray Donovan's resignation as secretary of labor in a Texas interview he thought wouldn't be attributed to him. I note that only to observe how skillfully White House staffers, anonymous to the last person, conducted their hidden war against Anne Burford until she was finally forced to resign as administrator of EPA last week. Again, these weren't small fry, nor were their identities all that hard to fathom. The president's repeated insistence that he stood behind Mrs. Burford was made a hollow mockery by men who stand at his side in most pictures.

But Mr. Reagan apparently continues to believe that the source of his troubles with leaks is to be found further down the chain of command. Thus, late last week came the idiocy to top all idiocies. He issued an executive order requiring every federal employee who has a security clearance to sign a nondisclosure pledge and agree to take lie detector tests when required. Failure to comply can result in "adverse consequences" and those who do not cooperate in leak investigations will be subject to mandatory punishment.

There is enough to prompt some civil libertarians to claim it violates the Constitution and promise a court test. But what it reveals about the president's willful blindness about the source of his leak problems is more interesting than the probable legal ramifications of a system which won't work no matter how toughly it is enforced. The rabbits he is hunting aren't out in the dark forests of the federal apparatus, but in the thickets right under foot. If he is serious about his statement in the new order that "safeguarding against unlawful disclosures of properly classified information is a matter of grave concern and high priority for this administration," he should fire at random every third person in his immediate staff. He would be more likely to hit the important leakers that way than by foraging out with lie detectors and FBI agents through Washington's teeming bureaus and departments.

That is said only partly in jest. To repeat the old saw, the federal government is a ship which leaks most profusely at the top. It is also an institution which tries to keep secret far too much information, with estimates running as high as 95% for material which could be made public without harming the national interest. Thus a president who is seriously concerned about protecting truly sensitive material would begin by making an example of those nearest to him who violate that concern, then pruning out that vast array of paper which doesn't deserve classification in order to concentrate more fully on the little which does.

But it is simply not serious to use a shotgun to go after a target which requires a rifle and to do so while expanding, rather than contracting, the classification umbrella. What the president is doing is a big, though bad, joke, and it's mostly on him.

November 3, 1983

The war in Grenada was waged much more effectively against the American people than against the world-wide Communist conspiracy the Reagan administration claimed to be challenging. We were deliberately and systematically excluded from direct contact with what was happening, fed grossly distorted information and, if not lied to in the simplest meaning, regularly kept from the truth. But no one should have been surprised. Since its first days, this White House has demonstrated in word and deed that it considers journalism to be as big an enemy as communism.

What has been more surprising, though barely, is the supine reaction of those who control the media. When they have not actively supported the president's amiable murder of the free flow of information, they have opposed it only in the most perfunctory ways. When they have not acquiesced with virtual silence, they have done so by the routine nature of their opposition. Another outrage against the people's access to news about their government, another resolution of protest passed, delivered and forgotten.

The indictment isn't overdrawn. To pretend that the owners of the broadcast and print media really care about Washington's war on openness in government is to fly in the face of the evidence. The old adage that a man's heart is reflected in the way he spends his money speaks directly to the reality in this case as in so many others.

Consider what the networks and the great media conglomerates do when something truly near and dear to their hearts is at stake in Washington. Certainly they pass their ritual resolutions and certainly they make sure that editorials are written and news events covered. Certainly, too, they send their representatives up to Capitol Hill to testify before congressional committees. But, unlike the situation when all that is at stake is the people's ability to know what their government is doing, they do not stop there.

If, for instance, they want a Failing Newspapers Act exemption from the antitrust laws, they spend millions of dollars and thousands of hours lobbying Congress, the president and the people on their own behalf. If they want to change the rules of the syndication game, they plot their campaign with all the care given to early morning assaults on hostile beaches and bring to bear their biggest guns for prolonged softening up of the opposition. There are no one-shot campaigns for the masters of the media when the subject is their balance sheets, and the results speak for themselves.

In the face of the president's clear, step-by-step progress toward the creation of an Official Secrets Act in fact if not in title, the occasional petitions for redress of grievance have been an ineffective substitute for the full mobilization of power. This White House reversed the trend toward less classification and more openness begun three decades ago and substituted lie-detector tests, pre-publication review for tens of thousands of current and former government officials, a restrictive approach to the Freedom of Information Act and administrative actions that make it increasingly easy to deny the people a full accounting of what their government is doing. At each step of the way, the president's men took stock of the media reaction, noted that words were never followed by action, and moved to the next turn of the screw, secure in the knowledge that those who mattered wouldn't respond in ways that mattered.

Now, in its handling of press coverage of the Grenadian invasion, the administration has made its intentions too clear for even the willfully blind to miss. It has emulated the British example during the Falklands War and gone a step beyond. But even in Britain, Official Secrets Act and all, the media rebelled, as detailed in a fine recent book by Robert Harris. Titled "Gotcha, The Media, The Government and The Falklands Crisis," it is a sordid but instructive account of what Mr. Harris calls:

"The instinctive secrecy of the military and the Civil Service, the prostitution and hysteria of sections of the press; the lies, the misinformation, the manipulation of public opinion by the authorities; the political intimidation of broadcasters; the ready connivance of the media at their own distortion. . . ."

In the same book, Mr. Harris quotes a speech given by Paul Scott Mowrer, then editor of the Chicago Daily News, during World War II. As Mr. Mowrer saw it, "The final political decision rests with the people. And the people, so that they may make up their minds, must be given the facts, even in war time, or, perhaps, especially in war time."

When King John encountered his barons assembled, they convinced him they meant business, and the result was the Magna Carta. When Ronald Reagan encounters the barons of the media, they convince him that they are complacent, overfed wimps, and the results are obvious from Washington to Grenada.

2

The Economy and King Canute

February 11, 1982

When the President talks, Americans listen. And when he warns us, as he did in Minneapolis the other day, that "in the days ahead, you're going to be submerged in demagoguery about the 1983 budget," it's time to look for evidence. As it turns out, we don't have to look far. Hear the voices of the "demagogues":

Sen. Alfonse M. D'Amato, Republican of New York—The budget is "totally unrealistic" and the proposed cuts in social programs would "bring about the ruination of the programs. . . . No comptroller in my town who came in with this document would have been permitted to work for me."

Gov. Richard A. Snelling, Republican of Vermont and chairman of the National Governors Association—"These cuts would fall heavily on many of the nation's needy citizens and would shift unacceptable burdens to state and local governments already struggling with the recession and deep 1982 federal aid reductions."

James Schlesinger, former acting budget director and defense secretary under Republican administrations—These are "a set of budget projections that knowledgeable people can only regard as preposterous. . . . One scarcely knows what this budget does for waste—but it does seem to have left intact generalized fraud and abuse."

So much for demagoguery. The president also warned us of another group of carping critics, the "paid political complainers." Herewith a voice or two from those ranks:

"We cannot accept a plan which jeopardizes the fiscal soundness of the states in order to decrease the federal budget"—the National Conference of State Legislators.

"Just read the history of the Depression, which started with the same policies"—Rep. Jamie Whitten, Democrat of Mississippi and Appropriations Committee chairman.

"Cutting another $400 million from aid to schools teaching the educationally disadvantaged—on top of the $600 million cut last year—is robbing us of our future."—syndicated columnist David Broder.

Quoting from other people is probably a cop-out. But before speaking for myself, one final quote about this budget, taken from Franklin Roosevelt's Second Inaugural Address:

"We have always known that heedless self-interest was bad

morals; we know now that it is bad economics. . . . The test of our progress is not whether we add more to the abundance of those who have much; it is whether we provide for those who have too little."

And that, in a nutshell, is what is wrong with the president's budget and his New Federalism. They would create and then lock into concrete a nation divided by class, race and section. They would guarantee a federal system comprised in almost equal measure of those states blessed by natural abundance and chance with booming economies and those states, economic losers for reasons of history rather than choice, mired in perpetual second-class citizenship. Rather than nurturing a more perfect union, they would instead produce a confederacy of inequality, in which the obligations of shared national community are submerged in the rush by states and individuals to beggar their neighbors.

Both, in short, are profoundly anti-democratic. Fortunately for the country, both are also excruciatingly unworkable. As everyone but the administration's hired guns say publicly, and even some administration officials admit privately, the 1983 budget in its present form is a smoke-and-mirrors joke. Where it is most honest—in the projected cuts in social programs—it is most disastrous in political and social terms.

Taken together, the budget and the New Federalism would give the nation a taste of the old approach to flood control along the Mississippi River. Before a national policy was adopted and implemented, each community and district lying along the river had one overriding objective when it came to high water. It was to build high its own levee and hope like hell that its neighbor's levee would break or the water could be passed just a little further south before breaking through or over the barricades. It was every place for itself, and the devil take the hindmost—and it didn't work.

That's why the federal government got involved in flood control and why there is a complex, interrelated system today which is heavily dependent on the U.S. Army Corps of Engineers. There was no way for the states and towns to do it alone.

What's true of flood control is also true of virtually every federal program put into place over the past 50 years. The Wall Street Journal's editorial stance notwithstanding, the past does not prove that "the best solutions to our country's problems usually come from the people on the scene, not from distant bureaucrats in Washington." What the past proves, from education to voting rights to highways to Social Security, is that the best solutions must involve Washington in basic ways.

The new budget and the New Federalism would, like King Canute, try to reverse that tide, but it can't be done without the kind of disaster against which Congressman Whitten warned. In the meantime, the quote which best applies to both Reagan initiatives was expressed by the little boy at the dinner table in the famous New Yorker cartoon:

"I say it's spinach, and I say to hell with it."

August 12, 1982

The problem with Reaganomics one year after its enactment by Congress is not only that it is a fraudulent failure in practice. It takes no bright-eyed child to point out that this emperor has no clothes. The more basic problem is that while those who promoted it may lose their intellectual and (if there is any justice in this world) their political shirts, too many other Americans are losing their pants.

It was particularly fitting that the first anniversary of the president's triumph coincided with the monthly employment figures for July. The new unemployment rate stood at 9.8%, another record for post-World War II America. Despite candidate Reagan's repeated promises to the contrary, the significant reduction in the inflation rate, which is the administration's only economic accomplishment, has been produced by the conventionally conservative technique of wringing it out of the hides of the country's working men and women.

The best way to think about Reaganomics is to consider the effect of malaria. Extremes grip its victims, with severely high fever followed by chills. The new economics ushered into existence a year ago is similarly a matter of extreme ups and downs. Among the ups:

The largest peacetime deficit in history, to be followed by yet another record deficit and then a third one almost as big.

The largest tax cut in American history, to be followed with the president's "total support . . . without any equivocation," according to a spokesman, by the largest tax hike the country has ever seen.

The highest number of business failures in 50 years, with the average for 1982 standing at 452 each week.

The highest-ever ratio of farm indebtedness to farm income, 12 to one.

That is a partial description of Reaganomics' fever. What of the chills—the lows—which it has inflicted on the country?

There were housing starts, which fell to a 35-year low in 1981. There was the automobile industry, which will see fewer cars this year than at any time since 1961. There was the value of farm land, which fell for the first time in almost 30 years.

Or, to think about those already afflicted by bad times, food stamp recipients will have to do with billions of fewer dollars. Those who need federally funded legal assistance and tuition loans and hot meals are going to have to scramble to make do with far less money. A number of other basic social welfare programs will be shrinking as the need increases. And that won't be all of it, according to Budget Director David Stockman. Even deeper cuts will be necessary in domestic programs in 1983, he told the Senate Budget Committee, if the administration's economic recovery program is to work.

Despite the stimulus to investment which was supposed to flow from the Reagan program immediately after its passage last year, many experts now predict that capital spending will be lower this year than last. Even the Commerce Department has lowered its earlier prediction of a 7.3% increase to 2%. Along the same line, the touted connection between deep slashes in marginal income tax rates and substantially increased personal savings has yet to be demonstrated in practice, despite the fact that many taxpayers in the higher brackets got the full benefit of the new rates immediately and therefore have had a year to put the proceeds to their intended use.

There is an answer from the White House of course: time. We haven't had a fair trial yet, Mr. Reagan says. Such revisionism is politically inevitable, but it doesn't square with the earlier pronouncements by the president and his men. In other days we were told that Reaganomics would go to work immediately to turn the economy around, that there would be a balanced budget in 1984 and, as presidential spokesman David Gergen said in July 1981, there would be no recession in the meantime. It was also Mr. Gergen who, speaking for the president, said that the economy would improve by the end of 1981, thanks to Reaganomics, and that unemployment this year would be below the 7% of 1981.

But press spokesmen are simply propaganda conduits. Closer to the center of administration rationalization, Treasury Secretary Donald Regan said just six months ago, which is to say six months after the 1981 budget triumph, that "the economy is going to come roaring back in the late spring." Six months before that, he said that the economy would turn up again "by the end of the year (1981)."

Well, that year has ended and this one is more than half over, and it turns out that Reaganomics is the modern equivalent of treating a very sick person with leeches. The quack keeps predicting success, and the patient grows weaker by the moment. The president asks for "patience from every one of us" as we "work our way back to prosperity." That isn't going to happen until someone pries the leech out of the body politic.

December 9, 1982

Economic idiocy is apparently a highly contagious disease. Just as it began to appear that the Republicans had recovered from their severe bout of manic tax cutting and defense spending, an illness which is an upside-down version of an old Democratic malady, leading Democrats embarked on what may be a lengthy cohabitation with protectionism. There is undoubtedly some immediate political pleasure in the process, but just as surely it will produce the economic equivalent of herpes. Since there is no justice in the world, moreover, not just the Democratic Party but everyone may have to suffer the consequences.

Former Vice President Mondale suffers from the most acute form of the Democrats' infatuation, although he has been saying of late that he has not really gone to bed with protectionism—yet. As he explains it, he is only threatening our old partners with this new infidelity so they will stop thinking they can take advantage of us with impunity. Or at least, that is what I think he must be saying, given recent columns by those favored with the latest chapter in "The Reeducation of Walter Mondale," a political tome which may eventually run to more pages than "War and Peace."

It plays well in Peoria, for the good reason that times are bad there, as they are all over the country. It plays well also because it is far more palatable to create scapegoats than to face facts. And it plays particularly well in some Democratic councils because major segments of organized labor have abandoned their allegiance to free trade with the speed which marked the steel industry's retreat from the same standard once foreign competition whittled its markets.

As the Walter Mondale of early October put it, "We've been running up the white flag when we should be running up the American flag . . . What do we want our kids to do? Sweep up around Japanese computers?" That's an approach which has everything, from a naked appeal to primitive nationalism to a not-very-subtle play on latent racism. And it finds resonance, as they love to say in Washington, in two recent actions in the Democratic-controlled House.

On Tuesday an amendment was added to the highway improvement bill which would require without exception the purchase of American-made goods for the $30 billion project. And the House Rules Committee on the same day cleared a bill requiring all cars sold in the U.S. to have a high percentage of American-made parts and to be assembled by American workers. In effect, it would close our doors to foreign-made cars. Presumably that would revitalize the auto industry, putting autoworkers back on the job and American-made cars back on the highways in the overwhelming percentages of the 1950s. Proponents argue that Japan in particular and other international competitors in general play similar games against us and it's time we got tough. "We've been played for Uncle Sucker around the world," a liberal New York Democrat, Richard Ottinger, elegantly put it during the committee debate.

Somebody's been played for a sucker, sure enough, and it's the American people. If these and similar measures become law, the net result at home will be higher prices for inferior goods, given the removal of real competition. But, according to the Congressional Budget Office and the administration, there would be no net increase in employment, but a likely drop.

That's because protectionism breeds protectionism. Each time one nation turns the screw, others reciprocate, responding to the same kind of short-term thinking and political demagoguery which has characterized much of the dialogue in the U.S. It would become increasingly difficult to sell American goods abroad.

The most vital sector of our manufacturing economy, even in

these depressed times, is the one tied to exports. Some 80% of new manufacturing jobs in America between 1977 and 1980 were related to exports. The success of those exports, like the success of our overseas sales of farm products, is directly related to efficiency, quality and innovation—attributes largely ignored for years in the industries now suffering most severely from foreign competition. While heavy American industry such as the automakers was concentrating on making a fixed, and relatively high, rate of return on an annual basis, the much-maligned Japanese were concentrating instead on expanding their market share by cutting prices and improving quality. Not surprisingly, Americans bought the better, cheaper products.

Now these industries, and their highly paid unions, want a bailout for their past mistakes, with all Americans paying the bill. That the bailout would spell only temporary relief for a small minority of all Americans doesn't seem to matter, any more than the likelihood that this localized relief would produce international economic indigestion and threaten the general health of the delicately balanced world trading system.

What does matter is that support for protectionism translates into money and votes for Democrats and a big leg up on labor support for the would-be Democratic presidential nominee perceived as standing toughest on the issue. But if the party follows some of its leaders on this issue, it will forfeit the right to reclaim national leadership. Protectionism, however slickly it is garbed and presented, remains a sick idea whose long-term effects could be terminal.

August 11, 1983

It is increasingly hard to remember, or to trust your memory if you do, that for a brief period in the late 1960s and 1970s there was a national consensus that no one in America should have to go to bed hungry. While it was Lyndon Johnson who launched and publicized the war on poverty, many of its most important components were expanded under Richard Nixon.

And while it later became fashionable in some quarters to claim that the war was a failure or a sham, accusations that came as often from the doctrinaire left as from the ideological right, the plain statistical fact of the matter was that millions of people were lifted out of poverty during the period, or had their plight considerably alleviated, by government programs and public expenditures.

Even when all the promises weren't kept, and programs proved to be flawed in concept and execution, the spirit of the effort convinced a lot of people that there was finally some reason to believe that things could and would get better, that the American dream was actually within their reach. Beneath the political hyperbole and exaggerated claims of utopia now, there was a clear, steady trend away from the majority's long and shameful disregard of the other, hidden America of hard-core hopelessness.

That should have been a matter of universal national pride, but for those whose feelings were accurately reflected by the New Right, it was a cause of concern. Big government was coddling the poor while soaking the rest of us, their argument went, and the experiment should be drastically curtailed.

The most prominent champion of that view was Ronald Reagan, and in the two and a half years of his regime, the government has moved vigorously to make good on his old campaign rhetoric. The fruit of its actions is now being harvested, although the farmer is busily seeking to disclaim either responsibility or intent. While administration policies prolonged and deepened the worst recession since the end of World War II, administration policy also cut back systematically on programs that might help compensate for the bad times. The official verdict was rendered earlier this month, when it was announced that the nation's poverty rate now stands at 15%, the highest level since LBJ opened war on the problem 17 years ago.

As always when faced with an embarrassment of substance, the White House decided to counter it with a flurry of propaganda and bureaucratic busywork. The president declared himself horrified at the thought of continuing hunger in America, vowing to "solve the problem" once and for all. Having made much of his unyielding determination to pare away or eliminate many social welfare programs, he now stresses how little has actually been cut. No longer emphasizing the need to eliminate chislers and cheaters, he now protests that no one has done more for the truly needy than he.

As one study after another has demonstrated, the claims don't stand scrutiny. People in need have been cut off the rolls. Programs for the poor have been reduced in critical areas. The spending figures look better than they are primarily because expenditures for entitlement programs that disproportionately benefit the non-poor have grown enormously. The administration has a clear sense of its constituency, and the poor are not included. But the media managers and campaign consultants who guide so much of what passes for policy in today's Washington realize that while there are few votes to win among the poor for this trickle-down president, there are a lot of votes to be lost among people whose sense of fairness is outraged by growing poverty at a time of massive tax benefits for the very rich. They sense that there is more than a little residual compassion among the non-poor for society's enduring victims. The task force on food assistance, announced last week, is only one manifestation of the determination to "reposition" the president, at least in the public's perception.

Which makes it important that the people remember former Attorney General John Mitchell's adage and look at what they do, rather than what they say. What has actually come of the administration's announced plans for inner-city development, for instance, and how does it respond to the importunings of the big-city mayors? What is being proposed to relieve areas of long-term unemployment such as the rural South or the industrial Midwest? What has actually been implemented?

The specifics are not the point, finally. What matters is a fresh commitment to the alleviation of poverty's worst effects, if not of poverty itself. The need is evident at every hand. President Nixon once said it was "embarrassing and intolerable" that hunger could exist in the world's most affluent country. It still is, particularly with recovery rapidly widening the gap between those in severe need and the rest of us.

November 29, 1984

What's going on in Washington isn't a serious exercise in budget making. It's the Reagan administration's version of the proverbial Chinese fire drill. The problem, however, is that the deficit is an ominous reality, not a circus make-believe, and the president's refusal to come to grips with its implications is not so much humorous as frightening. Add to the president's willful irresponsibility the additional ingredient that no one—underscore no one—in Washington today seems willing to venture a workable solution that stands the twin tests of fiscal responsibility and political feasibility, and you have the makings of renewed economic misery.

It all began with the long campaign, when Mr. Reagan rolled to an overwhelming triumph with an economic platform that was the intellectual equivalent of baby kissing. On Nov. 7, the kissing had to stop, and the barefaced liars who promoted the fiction that the deficit would be no more than $170 billion promptly started telling us that it would, in fact, total at least $205 billion, a new record. That was a suddenly "discovered" 20% increase, worse even than Walter Mondale and the Democrats had been saying it would be.

But what is the White House's official response to all this? As best as can be determined from what the president's surrogates tell us through leaks and contradictory predictions, it is as follows:

There is no problem, since the deficit will vanish in the face of sustained growth.

If there is a problem, it can be met by implementing the Grace Commission's 2,478 recommendations for reducing "federal waste."

And if there is a problem, no solution can include touching either the defense budget or Social Security, or raising taxes.

None of that has anything to do with the real world. It is Fantasy Island thinking. Even if it is not actually representative of what the president believes in his heart of hearts, it seems clear he has no intention of putting his political muscle behind any proposal that might require hard choices. Thus he allows the Treasury Department's tax-equalization plan, itself no answer to the deficits, to be released and then massacred by leak, all the while studiously distancing himself from any of its more unpleasant recommendations. His working group (read David Stockman) comes up with a plan to cut $100 billion from the domestic budget, and no one can be found in high places to embrace it and no one with an ounce of political savvy believes it stands a prayer of passage on its own.

Of course, up on Capitol Hill there is no rush to the standard of responsibility either. The slogan there seems to be, "It's up to the president," which is fair enough until you realize that everyone, Democrats and Republicans, congressmen and White House officials, is in the soup together, and it has come to a fast boil.

The dimensions of the problem must be restated repeatedly, if only to concentrate our attention. First, there is no chance that the deficit will be brought much below $200 billion a year without radical surgery. Second, no one of any political persuasion in mainstream America believes that the economy can sustain persistent massive deficits without buckling. Third, the program areas that Reaganite and Democratic electoral politics have put off limits total more than $700 billion of the trillion-dollar budget. The remaining $290 billion or so represents the money spent on everything except defense, interest payments and Medicare. There is no way to squeeze enough money from those remaining programs to lower the deficit by any meaningful amount.

Twenty years ago, Lyndon Johnson came out of his landslide and soon thereafter flunked the test of talking turkey to the people who had given him their trust. He decided he could repeal all the laws of economics and provide both guns and butter with no new taxes. As he saw it, we could have a war abroad and a Great Society at home with no pain and no sacrifice. The results laid the foundations for almost two decades of deepening economic malaise.

Twenty years later, Ronald Reagan is similarly playing King Canute with the tidal forces of the economy. The difference is that the budget is 10 times larger, the deficit is significantly bigger as a proportion of gross national product and the economy is already showing strain after a relatively short recovery. But, as in 1964, the problem arises "from the simple fact that most of us . . . want more from our government than we want to pay for," as Alice Rivlin put it in an Urban Institute study earlier this year. She went on to note that the president and his men hoped after the 1981 tax cuts and budget reductions that "some economic miracle would make these choices unnecessary. It was a miscalculation born of reluctance to face the unpleasant."

The unpleasant is now the unavoidable, unless we are to court disaster. The untouchable labels must be removed from defense spending and middle-class entitlements. A selective tax increase, preferably accompanied by reform of the sort proposed by the

Treasury Department, must be passed. The buck stops at the White House, but also at Congress as well. What's required is bitter medicine for Keynesians and supply-siders alike, but the patient can't recover without it.

October 17, 1985

The proposal by Sens. Gramm, Rudman and Hollings controlling and then eliminating the federal deficit is brilliant politics and appalling governance. It makes a mockery of the separation of powers, stands constitutional and political responsibilities on their heads and makes policy decisions by arbitrary formula rather than by a rational decision-making process. In other words, it accurately reflects the realities of Washington 1985. A bad idea whose time has come, it could well finally force responsibility upon those who have been resisting it like the plague for far too long.

The problem all along has been that no one would bite the multiple fiscal bullets that face the nation with lethal peril. Congress and President Reagan spent almost eight months wrestling with the budget, then compromised on a resolution that was divorced from reality when passed and has grown more distant from the truth of the situation ever since. It promises deficit reductions it can't deliver, based on economic projections no one accepts.

It's not that anyone disputes some basic points. The annual

deficit has quadrupled over the past five years, now averaging $200 billion plus each year. Thanks to the structural imbalances between tax base and spending so carefully created by then-Rep. Phil Gramm and company in the 1981 tax bill, there would be large deficits under the best of circumstances, so long as the president insists upon using national defense as the world's largest pork-barrel project. The circumstances, of course, were something less than the best for about half of President Reagan's five years in office.

And so the national debt—that sum of money we liberals once liked to say that Americans "owe ourselves"—has grown astronomically, fed by ever burgeoning deficits. From one trillion five years ago, it has doubled to two trillion dollars. Given annual deficits of $200 billion, give or take a few billion, by realistic projections it should reach three trillion by 1990. That money we "owe ourselves" is increasingly owed to others, and the transfer of national wealth from productive purposes to debt service can have only dire long-term results. It will sap the country's economic vitality and drive business and industry into permanent stagnation—or it will prompt the government to print its way out of one mess and into another.

So much for the obvious. Today, virtually no one disagrees that huge debt and large annual deficits are intolerable. But since the real pain and harsh consequences are in the hazy future, neither legislators nor the president has felt compelled to inflict tax or budgetary pain on their constituents in the here and now.

Into that vacuum came the appealing simplicities of Gramm-Rudman-Hollings. What the White House and Congress would not do for themselves, through hard choices among program options, the *deus ex machina* of annual, mandatory, across-the-board reductions would impose. All matters would be treated as though they were of equal worth, whatever their starting point and their utility. The just and the unjust alike would take the budget-reduction blow (save only that great untouchable, Social Security). Bloated or lean, each budget item would be cut by the same percentage to reach the pre-specified annual overall reduction.

And who would do the cutting? In the political sense, no one. If Congress and the president were unable to come up with a budget that reduced the deficit by the pre-established figure, then the act's unseen hand would take the president by the neck and force him to make the blanket cuts. Everyone would be to blame, and no one.

So much for sarcasm. Dangerously flawed, Gramm-Rudman-Hollings performs a major public service. It throws into clear relief the utter irresponsibility of both houses of Congress and the president. It exposes the collapse of the budget process, which meets its goals only by fudging them. It demonstrates that behind all the public protestations of concern about the deficits and the debt at both ends of Pennsylvania Avenue lies a great swamp of indifference. Finally, it creates a monster whose Frankenstein-style depredations should finally force consensus on intelligent alternatives to arbitrary, mechanical budget making by formula.

The matter is now before an extraordinarily large conference committee, the House having decided to punt into a huddle rather than try to advance the ball on the open field of play. As members of Congress read deeper and think more clearly, they may all find various reasons to alter the version of Gramm-Rudman-Hollings that the Senate passed. But some version will almost surely emerge, thanks to a fine mix of political shrewdness and political cowardice.

At that point, it seems clear to me that no one will actually find it possible to live with the measure over any length of time. Certainly not the president, who would be required to cut deeply into defense spending along with social programs. Not liberal and moderate congressmen, who would have to watch from the sidelines as the poor were even more severely penalized for their poverty. And not those in both houses who believe that Congress should be a live participant in the business of government rather than a mute observer of some clockwork process.

In short, Gramm-Rudman-Hollings will, like the executioner's ax, wonderfully concentrate the minds of those we have elected to represent us. Faced with the most unpleasant choice of all, which is to admit their irrelevance to the political process, they may finally make the hard choices and trade-offs necessary to confront the implications of our national sea of red ink. Having taken us into that sea up to our necks due to the economic policy mistakes of 1981 and beyond, they should finally be persuaded by their own legislative creature that they have the ability to repair them.

If that is wrong and if Gramm-Rudman-Hollings is called into play, it will fundamentally alter the shape of government and amend the Constitution through the back door. In that respect, it is a radical threat to our political system. But so, too, are the implications of the monstrous national debt. Given both, the president and Congress should finally be stirred to stop playing games and start meeting their basic responsibility.

July 24, 1986

"While some players may founder, the system shows no signs of sinking."—Time magazine.

There, in one smug phrase in the current issue, the heirs of Henry Luce encapsulated the moral myopia of most of the complacent, "morning in America" commentary that dominates the national dialogue. Even as the evidence grows steadily stronger that we are building a class-ridden society of ever-sharper contrasts between haves and have-nots, we are treated to long treatises on the triumph of capitalism and the American dream.

Time's neat phrase came in an issue that managed to ignore the single most significant piece of economic news of the week. The Census Bureau published a study that found that the net worth of the median white household was 12 times more than that of the typical black household and eight times higher than Hispanic households. While most of the stories we saw suggested there was no data available to make conclusions about trends, that is not literally true. In 1983, the Wall Street Journal ran a news story whose headline said it all: "Data on average wealth of blacks suggest economic gap with whites is widening."

That story quoted a study by the Joint Center of Political Studies, which was based on a 1979 Census Bureau study. The figures were not comparable to the new ones, because average rather than median comparisons were made, but they were comparisons with an earlier, 1967 private analysis that showed the absolute gap between white and black wealth to be substantially less.

Last week's Census Bureau report, incidentally, would never have been produced or made public if the Reagan administration had gotten its way. As the 1983 Journal story noted, the 1979 study was conducted under a program that administration wanted to eliminate. Congress restored the funds, and the Journal reported that later in 1983 "the government will begin collecting data regularly on personal wealth."

The result is last week's Census Bureau study, which gave emphatic credence to the Urban League's report on the state of black America earlier this year. As the league's John Jacobs put it, the report "describes a black America excluded from the economic boom, excluded from full participation in job growth and in danger of being excluded from tomorrow's economic mainstream as well." Black income, though better than the figures for black wealth, has been frozen at roughly 60% of white for 20 years. As a Joint Center for Political Studies research associate said, even after incomes are equalized, "it may be a couple of generations before wealth is equalized."

No one is holding his breath waiting for either the harder or the easier of the two to happen. But that is because there are so many other indexes today that strongly suggest that the America of assimilation, of upward mobility and of equalization of opportunity over time is becoming a thing of the past. Race is not the only determinant in the push toward the permanent creation of a two-nation society. Between the two booming coastal rims of the nation, near or on which over two-thirds of the population is destined to live, there is economic stagnation and despair. The agricultural regions of the Mississippi Valley are a wasteland. There is no meaningful revival in smokestack America.

Item: the U.S. Conference of Mayors this winter reported that in 1985, the third year of "recovery," the demands for emergency food, shelter and economic assistance were up "significantly." Some 85% of the reporting cities said there was an increase in homeless children.

Item: the Physicians' Task Force on Hunger in America stated late last year that hunger in America is "more widespread and serious than at any time in the last 10 to 15 years."

Item: the Education Commission of the States reported some time ago that 15% of youngsters between the ages of 16 and 19 are unlikely to become productive adults because of drugs, delinquency, pregnancy, unemployment and lack of education. About 2.5 million of them are "at risk" of becoming "disconnected" from society.

Much of this might as well be news from Mars for the majority of Americans who are not poor, not black and not young. For them, there is comfort in the data in last week's Census Bureau study showing that an astonishing number of Americans are living in solid, middle-class circumstances. And that is indeed good news about an almost revolutionary reality.

The problem is that we are structuring a country in which Third World conditions coexist side by side with prosperity; in which too few have far too much (12% of American households control 38% of all personal wealth) and too many have far too little. That describes many places, but not the American ideal. It is also social dynamite.

Three years ago, New York Times reporter John Herbers wrote something about the cities that applies equally well to the nation as a whole. As he put it:

"Despite a decade's hopes [and claims] of revival in the central cities, the cities became poorer and their suburbs richer. . . . With some exceptions, 'the other side of the tracks' is no longer visible to 'society hill.' "

April 23, 1987

Prime Minister Yasuhiro Nakasone of Japan arrives in Washington next week, long after the blossoms have faded from the cherry trees along the Potomac and the bloom from U.S.-Japanese relations as well. The president has announced a small set of economically meaningless but symbolically catastrophic trade sanctions, and a thoroughly buffaloed Congress is rushing to get ahead of the special-interest curve with trade legislation that ignores the lessons of the early 1930s. It's hard to think of an easier way to get a cheer from a Washington audience these days than with an attack on Japanese economic perfidy.

Which is more than a little strange if you look at the situation in nonpolitical terms. The $60 billion American trade deficit with Japan can be attributed only in a minor way to Japanese restrictions. The nation's overall $170 billion trade deficit last year speaks far more honestly to the root causes of our difficulties. Not too surprisingly, it is hard to find anyone who privately contends that the elimination of all unfair Japanese trade practices would change the balance by more than $10 billion.

But no one who counts looks at the trade deficit in nonpolitical terms. Since we live in a democracy, politicians tend to be political, and beating up on the Japanese is the moral equivalent of a free ride. It appeases popular passions and avoids confronting the unpalatable reality that we are the architects of our own disaster. Few officeholders ever won votes by forcing their constituents to look in the mirror to find the enemy.

The mirror reflects an unpleasant mosaic. There is the matter of debt. Personal, corporate, state and national are at an all-time high and getting higher. America is on a consumption binge for which it is perfectly willing to have someone else, in some long-distant time, pay the bill. Productivity growth, outside the relatively healthy 20% of gross national product attributable to manufacturing, has been declining. It fell from an anemic 1% in 1985 to an invisible 0.7% in 1986. The U.S. is now the world's largest debtor, with $150 billion owed and rising rapidly. Individual savings rates continue to fall and are now less than half the abysmal rate of 1980.

None of these figures can be attributed to nefarious Japanese practices, unless some assume that Tokyo has no right to economic vitality. Hard as it is to say and harder even to articulate in a political arena, we have been slipping into international economic trouble because we long ago got fat, dumb and slothful. We collectively decided that the great gift of World War II, our unchallenged economic supremacy, was in the divine order of things. Even if we had done everything right, even if we had run a lean, mean and taut ship on which today's pleasures were postponed for tomorrow's health, a slew of nations such as Japan and Germany eventually would have clawed their way back into competitive balance with us.

But we didn't do everything right. Arrogance, coupled with the delusion that what goes up may never come down, contributed to a precipitous decline.

Throw in a government that encouraged our worst instincts.

Throw in politicians of both parties who resolutely denied the truth of what was happening. Do all this, and you have set the stage for the current obsession with protectionism. It's patent medicine for a real ailment. While its ultimate effects could be fatal, it has the political benefit of tasting good as it goes down.

Someone is bound to be yelling, "There you go, blaming America first." So let's concede that the Japanese, along with a dozen other nations, have gotten well in part because we tolerated practices in the days of our hegemony that we can't tolerate today. They have also prospered in part because we assiduously helped them revive their postwar economies.

But the fault nonetheless lies basically in ourselves. As Gary Hart said some time ago, "Don't get angry, get competitive."

Behind the slogan lies bitter medicine. It means short-term pain for long-term gain. The American standard of living is already being crunched, but it should be crunched by deliberate choices rather than involuntary circumstances. Reducing the deficit, with emphasis on budget cuts in middle-class benefits as well as new taxes, preferably on consumption, is an absolute necessity. Wage rates, starting at the executive-suite level, must be restrained, with an explicit trade-off tied to shared benefits later from increased productivity and sales. While our society shouldn't even try to be like that of the Japanese, it can (and must) educate our youth as thoroughly as the Japanese educate theirs, which means longer school years and school days, and infinitely more parental involvement.

Edwin Reingold, a Time magazine reporter stationed for eight years in Tokyo, recently returned and wrote of the civility and efficiency he had come to expect in Japan. He came home to "bureaucracy, ineptitude, mean spirit and lackadaisy." Where, he asked, was the old American pride in competence, work well done and pride in service? Allowing for hyperbole, it is a question that arises in various ways, and until it is answered correctly, the threat from abroad will remain acute. It can't be answered by building protectionist barriers that lock inefficiency and incompetence into permanent place.

October 29, 1987

The international stock-market collapse is the supreme event of 1987. It is beyond hype, beyond glitter in that almost nonexistent territory of an event of real significance. The overnight elimination of a trillion or so dollars in stock values commands both attention and awed respect.

The spectacle of yesterday's insolent young masters of the market weeping copious tears of self-pity over their power ties is immensely satisfying to anyone mindful of John Kenneth Galbraith's famous dictum. To paraphrase his prophetic words, all that is required for genius on Wall Street is a rising market and a short memory. Having not very long ago been forced to endure the spectacle of Wall Streeters cheering lustily as President Reagan proclaimed the advent of the "permanent bull market," those with even a tiny sense of history have to feel a moment of barely restrained laughter.

But there are or should be several obvious checks on such sideline chortling by those of us who had begun to believe we had entered a wonderland in which none of the old economic rules applied. The first is that we are all in this together. That means those who are in the market and those who aren't. It means machinists as well as bankers, Germans and Japanese no less than Americans. As my father wrote in a somewhat similar time, the problem is that when "Wall Street loses its shirt, America loses its pants."

While that is not necessarily the literal truth in an era in which stocks represent a far smaller fraction of total wealth than they did in the 1920s and 1930s, and in which government policy and government controls provide far more safeguards and stimuli, it isn't entirely off the mark either. If the markets don't stabilize, the ramifications and multiplier effects could be very serious at best. At worst, they could be disastrous.

But there is another, somewhat less obvious reason for viewing the current situation with real alarm. It is that bad times, like the rain, fall on the just and the unjust alike. It is that the much-touted economic boom of the past five years has produced a misshapen society in which the poor have become both relatively poorer and politically less visible. It is that virtually all of the likely solutions to the problems reflected in the stock market will have the probable effect of making that poor minority even less politically relevant than ever in the next few months.

Dull statistics make the case about the continuing reality of poverty and its reach. The share of household income commanded by the poorest fifth of the population dropped from 4.1% in 1978 to 3.8% in 1986. The official poverty rate increased from a low of 11.1% in 1973 to 13.6% in 1986—and poverty for a family of four is an annual income of $10,609 or less. Compare that with the cost of a BMW, auto of choice for yesterday's market geniuses, and the figures come into focus. Remember that a fifth of all America's children live in poverty, and the focus sharpens.

Finally, a report issued this week by the Physicians' Task Force on Hunger claims that 20 million Americans do not get enough to eat. Economic growth "has not reduced hunger in any significant way. . . . The economic pie has gotten bigger, but the unevenness of that growth leaves millions falling further behind," the report says.

Even if everyone accepted this assessment, and many do not, what is being recommended as good medicine for the market's nervous breakdown could be poison for the poor in the short run. Reducing federal expenditures, so often promoted on the opposite page of this newspaper, will not come at the expense of the middle class. If you need to know why, look at only one other statistic. By election time 1988, about 90 million Americans who are otherwise qualified will not be registered to vote. A disproportionately large percentage of those 90 million are the poor, the young and the minorities, most of whom have either concluded with some reason that government does not work for them or don't care whether it does or doesn't.

But those who don't vote don't have influence, which closes the circle and leaves the poor outside when budget decisions are made. When they are made, the immediate beneficiaries will be those whose annual incomes are four times more than the national average, rather than those who live on less than half that average. And while economic vitality is a precondition, it is no guarantee of better days for the poor.

Almost two years ago, Sen. Daniel Patrick Moynihan said something that has resonance today and probably will have more tomorrow. "We are in a trough in social policy," he said. "But at least if we continue to focus attention on the data, we will be forced to think harder about what government will do when we get the chance."

Well, the data is still before us and the trough in social policy, the efforts of Sen. Moynihan and others notwithstanding, remains. What is doubly disheartening about the rout on Wall Street is that it virtually guarantees that the day when public and politicians alike will "think harder" about the poor will be postponed indefinitely.

3

Black America and the Candidacy of Jesse Jackson

February 5, 1981

For black Americans, the following phrase is bad history and bad tidings for their future:

"It is no coincidence that our present troubles parallel and are proportionate to the intervention and intrusion in our lives that result from unnecessary and excessive growth of government."

The words are from Ronald Reagan's Inaugural Address. They accurately reflect his basic political philosophy, which Urban League President Vernon Jordan well understood when, weeks earlier, he spoke of the profound shock and deep fear which the Reagan landslide had produced in the black community. Blacks, and other minorities as well, know that government "intervention and intrusion" helped them begin the long climb out of serfdom. The new census should provide depressing evidence of how much further they have to go.

Nor should there be any misapprehension about why they remained in bondage so long. The explanation is contained in a simple word, one which the New Left all but discredited by incessant misuse but which remains precisely relevant. The word is racism. The reality it encompasses is part of the fabric of American history.

The civil-rights laws of the 1950s and 1960s dealt directly, though gradually, with that reality, usually following the federal courts' lead but giving the courts' decisions lasting bite. Under their "intervention and intrusion," legally sanctioned and publicly glorified racism first retreated and then was shattered. Racially segregated public schools all but vanished in much of the South; all-white voting became extinct; black public officials became almost commonplace. Suddenly, the South seemed to leap from its position as the most segregated region to become the nation's most integrated. It didn't leap voluntarily. It was pushed by federal law and edict.

This brought the South to the moral plateau upon which the rest of the nation had long perched, and that brought the nation face-to-face with an unpalatable but unavoidable truth. The plateau was not very high. There was much to be done before the United States could say honestly that its principles and promises applied equally to all.

Two distinctly different factors then came into play. First, the economy began its long downhill slide, interrupted occasionally by remissions. Second, the federal government, thanks to President Nixon's Southern strategy, consciously turned away from its previous commitment to "intervention and intrusion" for racial equality. President Carter fought determinedly and often successfully to reverse the latter. He failed in his effort to reverse the former.

Statistics can be interpreted in various ways, but what cannot be ignored is that the dollar and employment gap between the mass of black Americans and white America has been growing again. Resegregated schools and segregated housing are the norm in too many places. The Klan's resurgence demonstrates that a familiar beast stirs again in the darkest recesses of the nation's psyche. Many white Americans are tired of conflict, of change and of hard questions. "What do they want?" they ask. "Haven't we given them everything they always asked?"

To which the answer is, everything except the basic requirement, which is acceptance as full partners in the American enterprise.

President Reagan spoke to that problem when he declared:

"Well, this administration's objective will be a healthy, vigorous, growing economy that provides equal opportunities for all Americans with no barriers born of bigotry or discrimination. Putting America to work means putting all Americans back to work."

Except, of course, that many black Americans, actively seeking it, never had the first opportunity to work. If the president's economic program is successful, employment for them will be a first-time thing, and not a matter of going "back to work." Many others got the opportunity not only for a job but for advancement primarily because of the government's "intervention and intrusion" on their behalf. They have good reason to believe that slackening governmental interest is at the root of their basic problems.

It wasn't many years ago that another president spoke eloquently in his Inaugural Address to the age-old American dilemma. As he put it:

"No man can be fully free while his neighbor is not. To go forward at all is to go forward together. . . . This means black and white together, as one nation, not two. . . . The laws have caught up with our conscience. . . . What remains is to give life to what is in the law."

The words were Richard Nixon's in 1969, which says something about the connection between inaugural rhetoric and presidential practice. They are worth consideration by the new president nevertheless. An improved economy is the *sine qua non* for everyone deprived of a fair share of the American pie, sure enough. But as over two centuries of American history prove, a growing economy alone will not insure a chance at that fair share. Federal "intervention and intrusion" are required as well. Perhaps more to the point, they are demanded by the Constitution and the law of the land.

April 7, 1983

The 15th anniversary of Martin Luther King Jr.'s assassination was marked by memorial services across the country this week, and that was just about all there was to it for white America and much of black America as well. It has been less than two decades, but in many ways those tumultuous, riotous days of the late 1960s might as well have occurred 200 years ago, so far removed do we seem from the passion and commitment of those times.

But that is a surface impression, misleading and finally wrong in its implications. The events of the 1960s and early 1970s had profound effects on the nation, forcing some changes and eventually fueling the reaction which culminated with the election of Ronald Reagan in 1980. The question now is whether the Reagan counter-revolution is the wave of the future, and, therefore, of a profoundly changed America, or whether the vast array of unfinished racial business from the late 1960s will set the agenda for tomorrow.

Mr. King's assassination came after he had moved his campaign away from a relatively easy task, that of forcing America to face up to the inherent contradiction of a South which lived by a code of white supremacy within a nation whose basic documents spoke to the equality of all men. It was not actually easy, of course, because never-never defiance went beyond lip service in the South and adherence to equal rights for all often went no further than lip service in the North. But as the late, great activist Al Lowenstein once remarked, the police dogs in Birmingham did have the salutary effect of selling civil rights in Des Moines, and the president and Congress responded to public outrage by pulling down the pillars of legalized segregation.

That brought the South up to the moral plateau of the rest of the country, and brought the nation up short. The plateau wasn't the mountain top, Northern claims to the contrary. De facto segregation survived in every region. The economic gulf between white and non-white was huge. Having a dream was common to all. Realizing the dream came very hard for most blacks.

Structural racism was deeply embedded and it would take a wrenching act of collective will to alter that reality. Toward that end, the civil-rights forces turned to fields in which there was no consensus: affirmative action and quotas, busing and guaranteed income. Mr. King was killed in the midst of a campaign on behalf of municipal workers in Memphis who were overwhelmingly black. His earlier march through Cicero, Ill., had convinced many Northern whites that he had quit preaching and, as the old joke had it, gone to meddling.

There have been advances since 1968 that shouldn't be ignored. But the finally dominant theme from Washington and the nation has been that enough is enough. "What do these people want?" is a common question. The failures of some of the new approaches, the anxiety of some groups as they saw their own cherished perogatives and accomplishments threatened by demands for what seemed to be preferential treatment for blacks, the bone-deep racism of others whose actions could be altered by law but whose beliefs were unchanged: all created a politically fertile field. The plowmen weren't long in coming.

Richard Nixon and the George Wallace of old spoke in different accents but to the same purpose. A Nixonian "Southern strategy" was intended to capitalize on the message which the Wallaceites wanted to send. The Carter presidency briefly reversed the trend, but with the election of President Reagan, Wallace and Nixon were merged and what had been subtle became overt. The new administration was determined to undo much of the work of the past and rescind the accomplishments of the Second Reconstruction. If that seems an unfair assessment to the president and his partisans, it understates the way blacks perceive his administration's words and deeds.

The tinder piles up. The gap between black and white grows.

A seemingly permanent underclass, outside the laws and the culture, fills our cities. The slide toward school re-segregation outside the South has become an avalanche. We are at least as racially divided as we were over a decade ago. Daily life for most blacks makes a mockery of the larger society's profession of belief in the Judeo-Christian ethic.

Lincoln notwithstanding, it is possible for a nation to endure half-slave and half-free. They so exist all around the globe. All it takes is force. But with our nation a new age was supposed to begin. If what is going forward in Washington, with the implied consent of a majority of the people, isn't repudiated soon, we should alter the Great Seal. The old dream, the dream not just of a black Southern minister but of the white framers of the Declaration of Independence, was what set us apart from the old world. We haven't lived up to the dream, but at least we preserved it, holding it out as the goal for all Americans. To watch this administration do its work is to watch the deliberate destruction of all that the dream proclaims. It can work, but it will take high walls and far more guards. It can work, but it won't be America.

April 26, 1984

Thirty-five years ago, it was possible to sing the line from "South Pacific" about having to "be taught to hate and fear" and go off into the sunset believing that the answer to racism could be found in education and positive thinking. Three decades of grudging, gradual but in many ways monumental progress later, it seems a quaint notion. Every step forward, to the side and back has been marked by immense effort, bloodshed, political turmoil and vicious resistance. In the collective national pause of the past few years, it has become clear that there is still a long way to go—which comes as a disturbing revelation to many whites, but is a basic fact of life for most minorities.

It is against this background that the current soul-searching about, and exploitation of, the presidential candidacy of the Rev. Jesse Jackson should be considered. The uproar of conflicting claims of "white racism" and "black racism," of media double standards and political hypocrisy, is not surprising. What is surprising is that anyone ever believed the nation would be spared a single moment of what has become an increasingly nasty debacle.

But first, a few misconceptions need to be cleared away. There is a thesis, popular in conservative and neo-conservative circles, that there is no longer really a racial problem in the U.S. There is just the problem of individuals, they like to say. The basic laws are in place and opportunity has been equalized. From here on, the race should be to the swift and strong—for everyone. It's a new way of parroting that lovely thought in "South Pacific," and no less simple-minded.

Racism is at the core of this society as it is at the core of almost every society known to man. The ruling group, majority or minority, tends to classify the subordinated group or groups as "the other," and to deal with those so classified in ways that set them apart. In setting them apart, subtly or overtly, the larger society announces that those who are different are also lesser.

Any nation, such as ours, that forces the vast majority of its minority populations to live in separate residential enclaves has already made clear how far it has to go to "put race behind it."

Similarly, any society whose most numerically significant minorities are largely grouped at the bottom of the economic pile is making a statement about race that cannot be ignored. And finally, any society that deliberately or casually guarantees that the vast majority of minority children will go to its most inferior schools is a long way from operating on colorblind premises.

And then along comes a black candidate for president, a man imperfect as all candidates are, and all these many strands are woven together in one candidacy and the reaction to it.

Long before Mr. Jackson made his utterly contemptible remarks about Jews, long before his racist supporter Mr. Farrakhan was emulating a long line of idiots in threatening destruction to those who didn't toe his racial line, Jesse Jackson's bid for the nomination was bringing out the worst in virtually everyone. The press and his opponents initially paid him the most demeaning insult of all, which was to suggest on the one hand that a black candidate should be treated differently (read more gingerly) than a white candidate, and on the other that his campaign should be covered like an entertaining but finally irrelevant sideshow. Opponents and friendly neutrals alike engaged in endless, mindless discussions about the "racially polarizing" effect of his candidacy, as though the races were currently existing in some vast blend of harmony.

All this until Mr. Jackson became a serious factor, able to mobilize a huge black vote in the face of opposition by more establishment-oriented black politicians who wished to broker their influence with one of the certain white winners. Suddenly he was the object of still more demeaning advice, focusing on the line that he should take care not to split the party by demanding "too much" at the convention. "Too much," of course, to be defined routinely by those who have given as little as possible to black aspirations in the past.

And then it turned out that a black candidate could utter racist remarks with as much ease and as little grace as any of the many whites who have been similarly caught out. (For that matter, until recently it wasn't a question of catching Southern whites playing the game. As Lyndon Johnson once remarked, crying "nigger, nigger" *was* the game in many states.) And all hell broke loose, as it should have, and Mr. Jackson managed to be as inept in backing away from what he had done as others similarly situated in the immediate past. A few people must still remember Spiro Agnew's "fat Jap" and Jimmy Carter's "ethnic purity."

If we had enough sense, we in the majority, we ought to thank Mr. Jackson for running. Not because he should or shouldn't be president, but because his candidacy has helped to put race and things racial back in public view where they belong. The hate, the contempt, the unyielding discrimination and the bland apathy are all there, as they have always been. At least now we are again looking them square in the face. It might actually help impel us to take up once more the deferred task of closing the chasm.

March 31, 1988

Once again, the workings of democracy have led supposed Democrats to premature and ludicrous despair. Jesse Jackson's extraordinary showing has bathed the party's small universe of movers and shakers in the kind of fear usually reserved for the outbreak of nuclear war. What they should do is view the startling transformation of sure loser to near-front-runner as a stirring affirmation of the openness of the American political system and the power of strongly expressed convictions.

Instead, they cower before the prospect that the eloquent black populist may actually be a dominant figure—if not the dominant figure—at the national convention in July. It is a ridiculous reaction for several reasons.

The most obvious is also the least significant in the long run. At the end of the nomination process, Jesse Jackson will be among the losers. He cannot and will not win enough votes to take the nomination.

He can't because his brilliantly conceived and articulated positions on many economic and foreign-policy issues are to the left of the Democratic, let alone the national, mainstream. He can't because his highly motivated base is too small, despite its fantastic rate of participation this year, to carry the day.

(Even in his best showing, he has not been able to muster much more than a quarter of the white vote, and this in a voting group far less burdened by overt or covert racism than the larger cross-section of a general election.)

And he can't finally because of the most important reservation of all. As Democratic consultant Bob Squier has put it, most voters are unwilling to offer the presidency as an on-the-job training program for a man who has never before held public office.

As Mr. Jackson would quickly reply, these negatives are the expression of one armchair analyst, whose vote is no more important than any other citizen's. But they are convincing to me and will be, I think, the operative factors long before July 18. For a man running to win (which is the answer to the question about Mr. Jackson's intentions), that is not a happy prospect. Nonetheless, he is already a major winner in vastly important and lasting ways.

For starters, it is likely that when historians assess the decade of the 1980s in America, they will decide that Ronald Reagan and Jesse Jackson were the nation's two most significant political figures. The reasons will be surprisingly similar. Both men know the value of sharply defined and articulated views. Both know how passionately most Americans respond to leaders with vision and commitment. Each taps a deep American nerve, one that throbs when old themes are invoked and old principles sounded. Each speaks to his followers' highest hopes and aspirations as well as to their angers and frustrations.

Even that is too negative a way to put it. Jesse Jackson's success in 1988 is testimony to the vitality of the American dream. Defying the odds and conventional wisdom, he has overcome obstacles of race, class and finances that not only seemed insurmountable a few years ago, but were. His achievement is the nation's achievement, a measure of just how far we have come in this second half of the 20th century.

It should be a matter of self-congratulation, not nervous clucking. Thanks to Mr. Jackson, black Americans will never again be bit players on the national political stage.

Nor has Mr. Jackson taken a conventional road to his present pinnacle. He has broken icons right and left along the way. His message has been consistent from section to section, week to week. No "re-education" for him, no "new populism," no periodic fine-tuning. He has been the one Democrat unafraid not only to sound many of the old notes, but add provocative new ones as well. He has embraced Yassir Arafat and saluted Fidel Castro, enraging those who would put a straitjacket on the public dialogue. Both acts, however, are sharp reminders of the sterility of much of what passes for debate about U.S. foreign policy. He has stretched the limits of what is politically permissible speech and that, too, is a great gift to a nation that prides itself on freedom of expression and opinion.

As for the complaint that his economic and social-welfare programs are ruinously expensive when not impractical, and that his gift for catchy phrases masks an intellectual void, one question inevitably arises: Compared with what and whom?

He does not even come close to the nonsense level of those who have campaigned throughout the land without offering a glimpse of their game plan to curb America's addiction to debt. What could be more fiscally irresponsible than the governmental record of the past 10 years? Are Jesse Jackson's slogans even a fraction as cynically meaningless as Richard Nixon's "secret plan" to end the Vietnam War or Ronald Reagan's "morning in America"? Is George Bush, the man of a thousand faces and no positions, offering anything of value other than "win one for the Gipper"?

Jesse Jackson has proved that a man with a message is more attractive than a man with a game plan. He has called into question the wisdom of the moral midgets who have been counseling the Democratic Party to shave its principles and accommodate itself to a sanitized version of the Reagan agenda. He has prodded Democrats to leave their hidey-holes, stop listening to the wheeler-dealers and start talking like Democrats again.

He has, to summarize, been about the business of redeeming the party. The notion that his strong showing, let alone his nomination, could lead to electoral disaster for the Democrats in

November is irrefutable evidence that his critics suffer from amnesia. No defeat in 1988 could possibly be more horrendous than those suffered by the party's nominees in four out of the past five presidential elections.

In reminding Democrats that the party's natural constituency is in the workplace rather than the boardroom, he is pointing the party toward a new majority status while forcing the faithful to remember why they were Democrats in the first place.

In short, it's time to stop nattering on about Jesse Jackson. The place to join the issue is at the ballot box. Those who want to stop him must and will do it there, or they can't do it at all. To do it, they must offer a message with at least as much appeal as his.

The enduring legacy of his campaign, of course, is that he has proved that his kind of message is good politics, and that's Jesse Jackson's finest gift of all to the process.

4

Politics in Reagan's America

November 13, 1980

There are disturbing signs of creeping moderation, if not downright nonpartisanship, in President-elect Reagan's approach to his new job. He should reconsider before it is too late, for the sake of his own credibility, as reassurance to his followers and, last, but hardly least, for the good of the country.

The tendency to rise above ideology will be encouraged by all the usual spokesmen of the received wisdom. James Reston has already advised victorious Reagan in so many words to look for good men from the opposition party and point toward a government of national unity. Arthur Schlesinger has reassured his fellow Andersonites that they need not fear the coming storm, because this is no parliamentary government and the new president doesn't have the stomach for a showdown anyway. Others have joined in the counsel of business as usual, suggesting that what the nation now needs is a new regime which relies on the old familiars from that permanent establishment which floats upon the surface of Washington like some ineradicable weed.

Which is all exactly what Mr. Reagan must not do.

He must not do it, first, because that is not what he was elected to do. His positions, blurred though they may have been in an excess of campaign caution, have been clear for a long, long time. They were clear to the majority which elected him. They were also clear to candidates for the House and Senate who said they shared his attachment to New Right verities.

There is, in short, a majority in place in two of the three branches of government (and arguably the third as well) to produce what the faithful legions have been advocating in the course of their long march back from the Goldwater debacle of 1964. (You remember, the election in which the Republican Party ceased to exist as a viable political entity, according to the established prophets of the time.) To snatch programmatic defeat from the jaws of victory now would be to betray all the effort and commitment and disappointments of nearly two decades of political toil.

For the new administration to fail to produce according to its own terms at last might be the final blow to the democratic process in America. It is already impossible to turn out more than a pitiful minority of the eligible voters for state and municipal elections, except in rare instances.

But the fact is that 52% plus did vote and a majority of those voting chose Ronald Reagan, a candidate who has made his credo well-known for at least 12 years. They did not pick a pig in a poke. There was no mystery about where he stood on the gut issues. Let him now make a mystery of those well-advertised beliefs, let him fail to attempt what he has promised, and the 1984 turnout will make the 1980 standard seem staggeringly high. Beyond that bleak prospect lies a dark and real shadow over the democratic process.

The President-elect has a responsibility to that process, to his party and to the people to make good on his rhetoric. He has the political resources to do so. He must not lose the will.

That means taking advantage of every appointment available to staff the Executive Branch with partisan, dedicated supporters. (Among the lessons to be learned from the administration of President Carter is the folly of "non-political" government.) It means being overtly and proudly political in the way the new President uses the powers of the presidency on the Hill and out in the country. It means pushing a program through Congress which speaks in substantive terms to the radical changes he promised in, among other things, tax policy and social legislation.

Above all, it means resisting the sweet blandishments of those who will attempt to convince him that what the nation needs is another four years of confusing mush, of government without ideology or perceptible principle. That is what the people believe they have had in the 1970s and beyond, and it is what they believe Ronald Reagan promised to foreswear. If they are disappointed yet again, they and we might as well begin looking for alternatives to our present system of government.

Nor should anyone kid himself about the way to read the tea leaves. A Cabinet full of retreads from the Ford and Nixon years will be a sure sign of creeping blah. A spate of editorials from newspapers which opposed Mr. Reagan, hailing the good sense of his legislative proposals, will be another.

Obviously, I have a deeper, and some might say, a self-serving motive for this advice. It has nothing to do with the textbook cause of responsive government, although I believe it is vital. Nor does it rest on the belief that the American people will really like in practice what they claim to have endorsed on Nov. 4. I am positive the Reagan approach to national and international problems will fall on its simplistic face wherever attempted.

But what seems equally certain is that if the new team decides to fiddle and faddle its way through the conventional ways, with the conventional leadership, the long overdue reassessment and rebuilding which faces my side of the political aisle will be postponed indefinitely. My side needs a rough, tough, mean and ideologically muscular adversary in power to regain our own strength and sense of direction. The liberal left needs to be faced by a head-on, mortal and consistent challenge to its comfortable assumptions and even more comfortable ways of doing political business in America if we are to show health again.

We need, in short, what the nation has needed for some time and what the people believe they voted into office: a choice, not an echo. If it isn't provided, we're all going to be in more trouble than anyone can imagine or predict.

January 24, 1985

There was a time, not many years ago, when most Democrats were fond of saying that it would be a cold day in hell before Ronald Reagan became president of the United States. Well, earlier this week, as President Reagan was inaugurated for four more years, it was cold as hell in Washington, but those consigned to the nether regions were men and women who once sneered at the man and his ideas.

Given the relative strength of the president and his adversaries, his foes should thank whatever political gods there be that conservative reaction to Franklin D. Roosevelt's enduring popularity produced the 22nd Amendment to the Constitution, holding each president to two terms. As of January 1985, Mr. Reagan is a colossus in a land of political pygmies.

There are two major reasons for his success. The first is that his policies either have worked (witness the booming economy), have not failed (Americans are not in an official combat) or have been quickly abandoned when they came a cropper (Lebanon). The second and more important is the power of his transparently heartfelt convictions. Confronted with a host of enemies united almost entirely by an abiding interest in power without unifying principle, he has won repeatedly by demonstrating that a firmly held idea will always fill a political vacuum.

In remaining true to himself and his ideology, the president has done what permanent Washington long ago declared all but unthinkable. While encouraging the silly parlor game of "is he or isn't he a closet pragmatist?" he has step by step advanced his basic beliefs until they are the overwhelmingly dominant agenda of the day. And it is Ronald Reagan who has done this, not the unseen Machiavellis who have been quoted so often in the news magazines as doubting their chief's grasp of facts or attention to detail. One of the more interesting aspects of the Reagan ascendancy is the closet contempt many of his closest allies seem to have for his abilities, as witness the conservatives' outcry over every staff change at the White House. Friends and enemies alike should finally accept one basic proposition: This is the presidency of Ronald Reagan, and just as the early failures were his, so is the latter-day ascendancy.

Shortly after his election in 1980, I wrote in this column that it was imperative that he stick to his guns and quickly make good on his implicit and explicit promises to those who elected him, while ignoring the condescending advice of the establishment pooh-bahs that he move promptly to the middle. The people, I said then, could not stand yet another betrayal of their trust. And, proving yet again that prophecy is not my strong suit, I said the Democrats should hope he would stick to his program because "it will fall on its simplistic face wherever attempted."

To be honest, I doubted whether this or any other president would do what I recommended. Rereading it, I'm struck less by its prescience than by the obvious fact that he didn't need my admonitions or those of anyone else to remain true to himself. Among my unsolicited bits of advice:

"The president-elect has a responsibility to that process, to his party and to the people to make good on his rhetoric. He has the political resources to do so. He must not lose the will.

"That means taking advantage of every appointment available

to staff the executive branch with partisan, dedicated supporters. (Among the lessons to be learned from the administration of President Carter is the folly of 'non-political government.') It means being overtly and proudly political in the way the new president uses the powers of the presidency on the Hill and out in the country. It means pushing a program through Congress that speaks in substantive terms to the radical changes he promised in, among other things, tax policy and social legislation."

The president did all that and somewhat more in his "new beginning," and now calls for a "new America." He has the political resources and the conviction to put flesh on the rhetorical bones of his second inaugural address. To put it mildly, I believe that many of the approaches he most ardently supports, at home and abroad, carry deeply divisive or dangerous long-term consequences. To put it bluntly, they would freeze inequality into near-permanence and much advance the transformation of this nation from a welfare state to a garrison state. The means he favors to advance the day of brotherhood at home and a nuclear-free world would almost certainly reduce the possibility of either.

But he is going to win another large chunk of what he advocates, barring a total change of luck, not because his position is so compelling or the specific programs he recommends are so popular, but because his opposition is so weak. Again, back on that November day in 1980, I wrote that "my side needs a rough, tough, mean and ideologically muscular adversary in power to regain our own strength and sense of direction." To reread this is to laugh. Rather than toughening up, much of the opposition has run for cover. That isn't the way Ronald Reagan got where he is today, and it isn't the way to defeat his ideas tomorrow.

For now, the calm, confident and supremely certain man who

inhabits the White House is master of all he sees. He got where he is the old-fashioned way. He earned it.

March 20, 1986

The president goes from strength to strength as chief of state and political icon, but the Reagan Revolution is over. Because he is so personally popular and because the Democrats remain so disorganized, both he and they may not fully realize the dimensions of this new fact of life, but its message can be read from Capitol Hill to the Pacific. Success, excess and the crushing weight of economic reality have combined to stop what was once predicted or feared to be the remaking of American government.

To say the obvious, the revolution managed to accomplish much before it ran its course. The rate of growth in many domestic programs was slowed. A few, unfortunately those that benefit people in real need among the working poor and children, were actually cut back. Government's regulatory role was diminished and in some cases ignored if not eliminated. Washington's official rhetoric took on a cast not heard for years, whether the subject was the threat to American security from Moscow or the threat to American capitalism from the welfare state. Finally, there was the defense budget; it ballooned in both absolute and relative terms.

But all of this is in the past. On virtually every front, the revolution is either on the defensive or in retreat. The president sounds the trumpet with all the old skill and passion. The troops who respond shrink perceptibly in number with each note.

Take defense. The day of budget-busting, pump-priming increases is over and a new era, which could prove to be equally senseless, of zero growth may be at hand. The buildup wasted more money in a day than a Boeing 747 full of proverbial welfare queens could have squandered in a century. The net result after Operation Blank Check is that every supposed window of strategic vulnerability is as open as it was (or wasn't) in 1980, and the people know it.

Take the budget generally. If Congress balks at the president's desire to jump defense spending an additional 8% or so, it absolutely refuses to slash still more deeply into most domestic spending. That is not necessarily a good thing, since the vast bulk of that spending goes for middle-class entitlements. A bipartisan consensus having apparently decided that those entitlements are sacrosanct, when the pendulum swings again someday the cutbacks will be even more narrowly concentrated on programs benefiting society's victims. But for now, the "big story" in Congress and the media is the resurgence of poverty in America. In the face of the newly rediscovered figures, the slogans of the Reagan Revolution are simply irrelevant.

As it turns out, that is the right word to describe the White House role in the current budget exercise. Democrats could be expected to proclaim the president's budget dead on arrival, and they did. But Republicans in the Senate have done no less, and their leading budget experts are today openly contemptuous of the administration and consider it a hindrance, rather than a help, in the hard task of dealing with the deficit. The advent of the $200 billion deficit and the $2 trillion national debt may indeed prove to be the most enduring legacy of the "revolution."

What will *not* is the now abandoned human-rights standard raised first by candidate Reagan, then carried forward by President Reagan's minions. The candidate repeatedly urged compassion for the world's right-wing dictators, asking that we "walk in their moccasins" before criticizing them, to quote one memorable radio talk. And so Reagan officials did, reflecting his United Nations ambassador's exquisitely sophistical distinction between authoritarian and totalitarian regimes. The president's first nominee for the State Department human-rights post advocated repeal of most human-rights laws passed by Congress since 1975. His first secretary of state said the war against terrorism would replace human rights as the centerpiece of American foreign policy. His policy of "constructive engagement" was more sensitive to white South African sensibilities than to black aspirations.

And now gone, all gone, swept away by populations that could not understand the hair-splitting difference between right-wing repression and left, that did not believe the choice was between a Galtieri or Marcos and communism. Swept away, too, by a Congress that in this field was and is far closer to gut American instinct than the hot-eyed architects of the temporary human-rights thermidor. The administration's scramble to get to the head of the column has required changing official policy without admitting it, as exemplified by the president's new definition of his human-rights stance earlier this month. Or if it isn't a change, it is at least old policy with a hypocritical new face.

More briefly, American behavior today in the international monetary marketplace is a repudiation of the ardent ideological free-market policy of just yesterday. Whatever, if anything, emerges from the tax-writing process may be reform, but it won't be Reagan reform. Environmental-policy debates are once again on how much to spend on such matters as Superfund and acid rain, rather than on whether such programs are necessary. Arms-control talks lag, but SALT II, that "flawed treaty" of Campaign '80, lives on.

There was a revolution of sorts, and like most American revolutions since the first one, it managed to change the nation's course within a much more narrow arc than most of the debate suggested. Now yet another course correction is under way, leaving the revolution in its wake.

July 3, 1986

"Ours is the only country deliberately founded on a good idea," John Gunther once wrote, and no one knew that better than that avid chronicler of the nation's byways and folkways. At root, it's the idea of liberty that has been fueling the joyful spectacle in New York this week in honor of the Statue of Liberty. And it's the idea, after all, that underlies all the fireworks and glitter of this and every Fourth of July.

But there are, as always, other ideas at work here. Just as there are tawdry aspects to the extravaganza in New York, there are forces in America that run directly counter to the precepts given prominence during this happy flag-waver of a week. They are forces the founders of the republic would have recognized, for they were known and rejected in their own time. That they are on the march again today should be a matter of wry, if brief, amusement, since they are at base the nostrums of unashamed statism, of totalitarianism wrapped in the banners of national security and morality. They are funny because so many of those who advocate them admit to neither hypocrisy nor inconsistency, even as they chant their battle cry of "Less Government."

Today, the Goliath of the State is starved at one meal, only to be fed double rations at the other two and snacks in between. At its simplest, this plain truth is illustrated by the fact that government is larger than it was when the Reagan administration took office. It costs tens of billions more, and it touches millions more lives. But that, we are instructed, doesn't count, because the emphasis of today's government spending is national defense rather than domestic welfare, and it is well known that the latter is infinitely more subversive of liberty than the former.

Perhaps, but the reallocation of resources to military spending has been accompanied by a reallocation of concerns at the highest levels of the federal government. If the old complaint was that government was too intrusive in the marketplace, the new reality is that government is too contemptuous of basic constitutional rights. James Madison might have been speaking of today when he wrote, "I believe there are more instances of the abridgement of the freedom of the people by gradual and silent encroachment of those in power than by violent and sudden usurpations."

Except that the encroachments have generally not been silent, and they have been gradual only because of sporadic resistance by Congress, courts, the media and the public. They have been unremittingly real, however. By executive order, administrative decision and public statement, the Reaganites have mounted a coordinated drive whose effect, professed aims notwithstanding, has been to speed the day when government of the people is replaced by government of Big Brother.

Put aside some of the better-known excesses. Ignore the assaults on the Freedom of Information Act, the executive order that enlarged the scope of classification in a country with millions of pieces of material already under government's lock and key. Overlook the use of the FBI to seize and examine the papers of journalists and private files, the exclusion of certain foreigners from the U.S. because of their views, and the expanding use of lie detectors in federal agencies.

Concentrate instead on the exemption of ever larger chunks of the federal budget from full congressional and public scrutiny. Note in particular that the "black money" (i.e., secret) category of defense spending has gone in six years from $4.6 billion to a proposed $22.5 billion. That's a jump to 7% from 3% of the military budget. Add that to the publicly unacknowledged billions hidden in the overall budget for intelligence functions, and you have a government disturbingly free of normal checks and balances—and government closer to Soviet norms than American. "Trust us" becomes the byword, and this in a nation that prides itself on a government of laws rather than of men.

It is possible for the public to ignore CIA Director William J. Casey's exercises in press intimidation and public calls for prosecution of news organizations for supposed breaches of national-security laws. Let the press look after itself. But what of the rapid government centralization of personal data banks in marked disregard of Privacy Act restrictions?

And what, too, of the slimily effective methods of the staff of the attorney general's pornography commission? Its executive director wrote to a number of companies noting that the commission had heard testimony (from one person, actually) that they engaged in the sale and promotion of pornography. He suggested they had an "opportunity" to take steps before their names were listed in the commission's final report as purveyors of filth. Some thought they understood the message and removed Playboy and Penthouse, among other magazines, from their shelves. No loss to literature, perhaps, but a great loss to freedom, with the government playing the role of inappropriate censor.

Speaking of the possibility of such trends 30 years ago, the late Supreme Court Justice William O. Douglas said: "These short cuts are not as flagrant, perhaps, as a lynching. But the ends they produce are cumulative, and if they continue unabated can silently rewrite even the fundamental law of the nation."

Those are good words to remember this week between the fireworks and the Elvis look-alikes.

August 14, 1986

Let us start with a proposition with which most, or at least many, Americans agree. Drugs are a serious problem in our nation's life, the "American disease," as Dr. David Musto termed it in his 1973 book. Let us further agree that illegal drugs are an epidemic that "has taken lives, wrecked careers, broken homes, invaded schools, incited crimes, tainted businesses, toppled heroes, corrupted policemen and politicians, bled billions from the economy and in some measure infected every corner of our public and private lives," as Newsweek editor-in-chief Richard M. Smith put it in the June 26 [1986] issue. And finally, these points having been made, let us all acknowledge that it is both inevitable and right that politicians from the president on down would try to get to the head of public concern by launching national campaigns against illegal drugs.

But there is a weird lack of proportionality in all this, for a reason I will try to make clear further on. First, however, some facts and figures about addiction in contemporary America.

One addictive "drug," legal in every state, claims 350,000 lives a year. It is used by some 55 million Americans, 85% of whom say they would like to quit and 61% of whom have tried and failed. It is promoted by one branch of government, subsidized by another and opposed by yet another. Advertised widely and, for the most part, misleadingly, it is targeted increasingly at younger adults—and women in particular. It is, of course, tobacco.

Another "drug," also legal in every state, kills an estimated 100,000 people a year. Used by perhaps 115 million Americans over 18 and the drug of choice for teen-agers, it produces 10 million to 12 million addicts and severely cripples their health and occupations. It is alcohol.

Finally, there are those substances more commonly referred to as drugs: cocaine, heroin, PCP and the like. According to the National Institute of Drug Abuse, these substances were implicated in 3,562 deaths in 1985, of which 643 were tied to cocaine and 1,315 to heroin. There were just over 100,000 hospital emergency-room mentions for drugs in 1985.

Estimates of the costs to society of each of the three categories vary widely, but according to the experts, there are some useful approximations. They say that smoking costs might have been as high as $95 billion last year. The societal cost of alcohol was put at $116 billion in 1983. And in the same year, an updated study claims, drugs cost society some $60 billion. These estimates include such things as lost or reduced productivity, hospital or medical treatment and criminal-justice costs.

In other words, in every measurable category, alcohol and tobacco are today infinitely more harmful to the nation and its people than illegal drugs. In every measurable category, that is, save one, but that one is of immeasurable importance. The illegal drug trade today is corrupting government, subverting the legal system and fashioning an invisible empire that rivals legitimate enterprises in every area of economic life. South Florida today makes the Capone-era Chicago look like a model of civic rectitude. The profits from illegal drug trafficking generate billions of dollars, billions that submerge and then absorb banks, billions that buy judges, businesses, real estate and the ears of the politically powerful—if not their souls.

That puts these drugs in a special category, but it is a category made special by the law itself. Change the law, and you narrow the problem to its health component. Repeal today's version of prohibition, in other words, and you are free to spend the sums now going into failed law enforcement on the vastly more important areas of scientific research and public education. Decriminalization is not offered because of a belief that such drugs are benign. Decriminalization is necessary to stop and then eliminate drug-trade-generated corruption so that government and society can concentrate on reducing consumption.

Happily, all is not gloomy on that front. The number of drinkers is decreasing, though there are disturbing signs of an increase of alcoholism among young Americans. The percentage of Americans who smoke continues to decline. Concerted campaigns on both fronts by private and public organizations have been largely responsible, as has been the vastly increased pool of scientific information on the pitfalls of both smoking and drinking.

Gone, too, are the days of ignorance masquerading as sophistication, when decriminalization was advocated because "recreational" drugs were said to be risk free. They aren't. Some have the immediate, malign impact of a bullet. Others take longer to kill and maim. Virtually all have medical side effects whose consequences are just becoming clear.

But the tasks at hand should be differentiated. The serious, costly business of public education should be separated from the inevitably futile and infinitely more costly efforts to impose abstinence by law. As Dr. Musto has pointed out, American drug abuse comes in cycles. Each "cycle started with extreme enthusiasm, then uncertainty, then a feeling that this is an extremely dangerous substance," he told the Los Angeles Times.

And that is where we are with cocaine, heroin and similar destructive drugs today, and with tobacco and alcohol as well. The objective should be to remove the promise of huge profits from illegal drugs by legalizing them, and spend more to intensify public awareness of the dangers in all forms of "the American disease."

September 18, 1986

The nominations of William Rehnquist and Antonin Scalia are ready for the history books, and it's to history that we should turn while considering what, if anything, the sound and fury have been all about. As usual, even limited familiarity with the past makes it impossible to view the present from the perspectives offered by the deadly serious debaters on both sides. What is most interesting about the Supreme Court showdown and the underlying cleavage over the proper role of the court is the way that ideological enemies have totally reversed their positions over the past half century.

At root, Messrs. Rehnquist and Scalia are happy to be known as apostles of the philosophy of judicial restraint, and their liberal opponents are equally eager to credit them with just that legal stance. Conservatives claim that is the way to stability. The left says in effect that it dooms society to sterility and reaction. Both are masking what is really at stake.

Fifty years ago, the shoes were on different feet. The most eloquent speeches ever given in favor of strict constitutional constructionism were being offered up by Franklin Roosevelt. The Supreme Court had been striking down some of his pet New Deal measures in ardently activist fashion, as indeed a conservative Supreme Court had been doing against state legislative innovation in the social and economic welfare areas for decades, and the president thought he knew the answer: Bring the court to heel by packing it with additional members more in tune with the popular will.

Liberals enthusiastically agreed, but the Senate Judiciary Committee thought otherwise: In reporting out his court-packing bill with a negative recommendation, the committee majority said: "Let us, of the 75th Congress, declare that we would rather have an independent court, a fearless court, a court that will dare to announce its honest opinion in what it believes to be the defense of the liberties of the people, than a court that, out of fear or sense of obligation to the appointing power, of factional passions, approves any measure we may enact. We are not the judges of the judges. We are not above the Constitution. . . ."

Thus spoke a conservative majority, echoing in its own way the sentiments of the very conservative Chief Justice Charles Evans Hughes some 30 years earlier. He declared: "We are under a Constitution, but the Constitution is what the judges say it is, and the judiciary is the safeguard of our liberty and of our property under the Constitution."

The chief justice knew whereof he spoke. The Supreme Court had only recently, without discernable congressional intent or guidance from the plain language of the amendment itself, decided to "safeguard" property by defining corporations as persons under the terms of the 14th Amendment. It was "loose constructionism" with a vengeance, heartily cheered then as now by conservatives who admired the result.

Liberals railed against just such judicial activism for decades, until changing tides of fortune produced the long Democratic hegemony. Federal court rulings began to prove the truth of Mr. Dooley's adage that "th' Supreme Court follows th' ilicition returns," if not precisely in the way he had meant it. The federal bench was reshaped by the power of appointment during the Roosevelt-Truman era to reflect a new philosophy. The court was "democratized," and its activism began to cut a different way.

The change in the frame of reference promptly, and unsurprisingly, produced a flip-flop in ideological positions. Liberals became the sycophantic supporters of everything that the least democratic of the three branches of government brought forth, since it was carrying their water. Conservatives, conversely, began to preach piously about the necessity of trusting the legislative process to cure societal ills. The courts, they said without even the trace of embarrassment, should not "make law."

But it was the left that was constructing its own petard. Changing political fortunes lit the fuse. If a new era of conservative control is not yet guaranteed, the past five presidential elections have given a strong clue to its imminent possibility. Soon it will be a Nixon-Ford-Reagan court, from top to bottom. Just how far down the broom will sweep can be seen in the fact that Lyndon Johnson was the last Democratic president to name a Supreme Court justice, while Ronald Reagan alone will have appointed at least 40% of the nation's 752 federal judges before he retires.

The president and conservatives speak of the need for "strict constructionism," of course, of judges who will respect the Constitution and the will of the people. The echo you hear is Franklin Roosevelt. What William Rehnquist has demonstrated repeatedly, and what many conservatives hope is coming, is that the slogan masks judicial activism that simply marches to a different and older drummer. What goes around, comes around. And for the liberals today, in the wake of Messrs. Rehnquist and Scalia, and their like-minded colleagues to come, their next step is to be found (as for the conservatives before them) in the words of that famous constructionist, Justice Felix Frankfurter:

"In a democratic society such as ours, relief must come through an aroused popular conscience that sears the conscience of the people's representatives."

Until then, the court will, as usual, follow the election returns, ad infinitum.

April 2, 1987

Context is everything. Without it, this week's loudly ballyhooed showdown between the president and the Democratic Congress over the interstate-highway construction bill would have been well-nigh inexplicable. The president's propaganda notwithstanding, the $87.5 billion measure really wasn't a budget-buster, and everyone knew it. The Democrats' keening to the contrary, they could have compromised earlier, guaranteeing a major public-works program for the summer that would have covered almost all the necessary bases.

But compromise was not what either side had in mind. For the president, the time had come to draw a line in the dust, take off his jacket and pick a fight. Having been in retreat from the time of the Iceland summit and the congressional elections to this spring, he and his closest advisers clearly decided they had to prove to the Democratic majority on the Hill that he was still king of the mountain.

For the Democrats, the reverse was equally true—but something else was also at work. Having watched the government's investment in infrastructure, education and civilian development steadily and sharply cut over the past six years, the Democrats decided the time had come for an all-out counterattack. By virtually every indicator of public opinion and national need, they are on firm political ground.

While some may try, it is hard to argue that the nation's roads, highways and other basic capital stock are not in seriously deteriorated condition. The hard rain in Washington early this week managed to camouflage temporarily the thousands of potholes that stretch through the city like petite canyons, but they didn't save us, the motorists, from feeling their presence. And what is true in Washington is writ large in New York, New Orleans and dozens of other American cities. Fancy new hotels and office buildings, monuments to a boom economy that has made the affluent more affluent while leaving the poor ever more separated from the mainstream, rise above pockmarked roadways that mock the very idea of progress.

As for the interstate system, that monument to intelligent Republican foresight when launched by President Eisenhower more than three decades ago, it is crumbling before our eyes. In his new novel "The Thanatos Syndrome," Walker Percy alludes to that reality: "A short hop, but the old interstate, broken and rough as it is, is nevertheless clogged with truckers of all kinds, great triple tandems and twenty-six wheelers thundering along at eighty who like nothing better than terrorizing private cars like my ancient Caprice."

Name a sector of the economy or the nation in which federal investment has been central to development and growth, excepting only spending for national defense, and the picture is the same. The new federal budget would take more than $3 billion out of aid to education, a reduction of more than a sixth of last year's figure. That cut comes on the heels of severe slashes throughout the rest of the 1980s and in the wake of repeated studies of education that suggest that we need more, not less, investment in this basic element of national infrastructure. Housing as a federal function has ceased to exist in all but name, and the results can be seen in the swelling ranks of the homeless and the overnight disappearance of adequate shelter for poor Americans.

A few years ago there was a concentrated burst of rediscovery by the media of how bad conditions in the public sector had become. Remember all those horror stories about sewer and gas lines collapsing beneath city streets and bridges becoming unsafe at any speed? The stories are gone, but the conditions remain virtually unchanged where they are not worse. Deferred maintenance and reconstruction are adding up to huge liens on the future.

But there is another context for all this, created by the administration's irresponsible fiscal policies and then cited by the administration as the rationale for rejecting a renewed commitment to Washington's historic role in nation-building. That context is the mountain of debt the president has given us as his most enduring legacy. Because of the huge deficits that tax cuts and defense pump-priming have produced, and because of the trillion-dollar addition to the national debt those deficits have created, there seems to be little leeway for capital projects for civilian use.

Which leads to a final context. Congress and president have joined to enshrine middle-class entitlements as the sacred cow of the budget-making ritual. While Congress has finally regained its equilibrium on defense spending, it has yet to measure up to its responsibility to reform and reshape all transfer and entitlement programs, beginning with Social Security. It is, sadly enough, Congress's responsibility alone for the simple reason that the president has repeatedly demonstrated that he is no more likely to grasp that nettle than to face up to the need for a tax increase that is called a tax increase.

And the reason, at root, for all those failures is that this president, in the seventh year of his presidency, has no more understanding of the government's paramount responsibility to keep the nation's framework healthy than he did in his first. As in the interstate-highway fight, he is more concerned with old slogans than pressing national needs. That must be remembered as he and Congress confront each other in the coming months.

January 28, 1988

The president gave a bravura performance in his State of the Union address Monday night. He ran the old standard up the flagpole one more time, and just about everyone saluted. The problem, as became clear on a close reading of what he actually said as opposed to how he said it, was that he was using a 13-star flag in a 50-star world.

Two phrases—which are elided into one below—from the address establish how removed he is from the reality of his own making:

"Let's be clear on this point: We're for limited government because we understand, as the Founding Fathers did, that this is the best way of ensuring personal liberty. . . . As I indicated in my first State of the Union, what ails us can be simply put: the federal government is too big and spends too much money."

There are those who believe he is right on both counts. I don't. But whatever the virtues of the rhetoric, in practice this president has presided over the steady growth of government and the continuing accretion of real power in the hands of the state. That he has done so despite monumental, and monumentally successful, assaults on the role of the federal government as the comforter of the afflicted only underlines the point. What Ronald Reagan has done is shift the discretionary budget emphasis of this domestic republic from social welfare to military expenditures.

Furthermore, while guiding that historic shift, he has refused to pay for what he was doing. The result has been more people working for Washington rather than fewer, a disastrously swollen national debt and a federal government—and economy—unhealthily centered on military spending.

Take a few figures. In 1981, there were about 2.85 million federal civilian employees. Today, the figure is just over three million, a 7% increase. During the same period, the number of Defense Department employees went up by more than 10% while the non-defense work force was dropping. By 1987, there were virtually as many civil servants working for Defense as for the rest of the government outside the Postal Service. Equally of note, there are another three million people who work directly or indirectly for the Defense Department in private firms.

Meanwhile, the decline in other U.S. agencies' employment has included: Interior Department, 14%; Commerce Department, 11%; Health and Human Services, 17%; Housing and Urban Development, 28%; Transportation, 18%. Those squeezes have taken place while the president was pouring just short of $2 trillion into the military budget. The only reason the tilt was not more pronounced was that Congress occasionally balked.

Even with that resistance, however, a fearful toll has been taken both on the nation's infrastructure and its basic human needs. All the while, the government has been growing in every way except one: the capacity and willingness to pay for what it was doing. That, too, was a matter of presidential decision, since not one of his proposed budgets in seven years would have put the nation even close to the black.

Thus there was a moment of unconscious irony Monday night when the president rang the tocsin about a fourth of the way through his speech, suggesting that "perhaps the most important sign of progress has been the change in our view of deficits." His apparent point was that everyone, liberal as well as conservative, is now terrified by the Reagan record deficits and his $1 trillion addition to the national debt. But someone else might have read it to mean the president's own blithe disregard of the meaning of those deficits and that debt, a truly significant change in a politician who once ran against both.

A recent book by Paul Kennedy, whose abbreviated title is "The Rise and Fall of the Great Powers," drives home one lesson with awesome repetition and numerous examples: The history of great powers is marked first by economic dynamism that takes them to the top, then decline caused by mounting military burdens that erode and then destroy the economic base that first created the power.

But this analysis is in the book stores in 1988. In 1956, President Eisenhower shared with a friend his concerns about the tendency of the military services to ask for more than they needed and the economy could sustain. He wrote in part:

"Let us not forget that the Armed Services are to defend 'a way of life,' not merely land, property or lives . . . [and what is needed is] balance between the minimum requirements in costly implements of war and the health of our economy. . . . But someday there is going to be a man sitting in my present chair who has not been raised in the military services and who will have little understanding of where slashes in their estimates can be made with little or no damage. If that should happen while we still have the state of tension that now exists, I shudder to think of what could happen in this country."

Shudder no more. Ike, meet the Gipper.

April 21, 1988

The New York primary has eliminated the suspense about the Democratic nominee. The terrorists have released their hostages from the Kuwaiti airliner. And the Persian Gulf seems to have gone from Condition Red to Condition Yellow. That means citizenry and government can concentrate on the half-dozen or so other issues that seem to defy solution or promise new headaches.

What we're talking about here are not headaches caused by embarrassment. In that category are the continuing scandal of Edwin Meese's hemorrhaging Justice Department and the temporary scandal of Larry Speakes's admission of practices different only in degree from those routinely followed by his counterparts past and present. (Washington journalists ought to be embarrassed by their hypocritical mewling about Mr. Speakes, since most of them have long been willing co-conspirators in the daily frauds perpetrated on the public by the government's $2 billion-a-year "public-information" industry. Journalists' capacity for moral outrage is remarkably limited when it comes to their own defects.)

What we are talking about is best summarized by reference to April's headlines. There have been so many that most of us have simply taken vows to quit thinking about public affairs altogether and, in the best tradition of the 1950s, cultivate our own gardens.

As with the 1950s, ignoring the mounting difficulties will not solve them. To its credit, the Reagan administration has proved on a number of fronts it has learned that lesson, whatever the president's ideological preferences might be. Thus Secretary of State Shultz engaged Israel and its neighbors in a game, if futile, effort to resurrect the Mideast peace process. The assassination of the PLO leader and the mounting outrages in the name of law and order on the West Bank and in Gaza underscore a deadly reality: Until there is an agreement satisfactory to all parties, there will be peace for none.

It has not been for lack of administration attention that another war has failed to produce adequate results: the war for stability in the international economy. Debt is still the doomsday bomb: debt owed by Third World nations to the West and by Americans to everyone at every level of economic engagement. Washington's efforts have been severely hampered by self-imposed political restraints on so much as discussion of possible options. The result has been half-way measures that reassure no one and fix little. The dollar's continued fall and the market's extreme volatility are but thermometer readings of a raging fever.

No one can argue that Americans from top to bottom are ignoring the drug problem. Politicians are as one in their commitment to attacking the menace of crack and other "hard" drugs. Polls show the public believes hard drugs are the leading menace to the nation. There will be immense pressure on the next president to "do something." What should be argued is that the focus is all wrong, that hard-drug addiction is far less the problem than the crime and corruption that hard-drug prohibition has produced. Until that message sinks in, we will continue to lose the "war on drugs," just as we lost the war on alcohol in the 1920s.

If drugs are the problem of choice, the widening gap between the very poor and the rest of us is the problem virtually everyone prefers to ignore. It is not a racial issue, though blacks and Hispanics are disproportionately represented in the poverty class. It is not simply a law-and-order issue, though the gang wars in Los Angeles remind us every day of the reality that Americans live in incredibly different worlds shaped in large measure by economic opportunity.

It is entirely a moral and political issue, however, calling into question our faithfulness to our democratic heritage and its future. This has long been a society divided between the "haves" and the "will haves," to steal a phrase. When the day arrives that class lines grow rigid, when we are a nation of permanent haves and have-nots, we will have become something other than America.

Finally, as stories from Panama, Honduras and Nicaragua make apparent, the U.S. has not come to grips with the limitations on the use of national power in the world. The Soviets' retreat from Afghanistan underscores the point. It is far easier to impede imposition of external power on a country than to impose it. The Brezhnev and Reagan doctrines are as one with the Colossus of Rhodes, reminders of a fast-receding age. But America's power nonetheless carries leadership responsibilities if the world is to remain at least minimally hospitable to our interests and security. The trick, yet to be mastered, is to devise a foreign policy embracing both realities.

This short list illustrates the kinds of issues the parties' presidential nominees should debate in the fall campaign. The temptation to pander on the one hand or ignore on the other will be almost overwhelming. But the person elected will have to confront them all. It will be far easier to enlist the people in proposed solutions if they have already been engaged in a meaningful debate on those solutions. Sliding through to victory on platitudes makes sense right up until the day after the inauguration.

Part Two

THE FOREIGN SCENE

1

The Playing Fields of Central America

March 19, 1981

Aside from the fact that it has been gloriously inept, there is nothing particularly unusual about the Reagan administration's attempt to fine-tune the press accounts of its anti-Communist crusade in El Salvador.

Every administration suffers from the delusion that the press exists to run its handouts on delivery and stop running them on demand.

Thus when some officials in the upper reaches of government

decided last week that the growing emphasis on a possible "new Vietnam" was not useful, they reacted according to an old script. They sent an errand boy out to stage a backgrounder dedicated to the proposition that coverage of the developments relating to El Salvador was being overdone.

"This story has been running five times as big as it is," acting Assistant Secretary of State John Bushnell told a group of diplomatic correspondents, "and we figured that if we talked to you about it, you might not make this thing such a big deal."

Backgrounders by assistant secretaries do not just happen. They are carefully cleared from above. That made it a little out of the ordinary when White House Press Secretary James S. Brady, after an interesting pause of several days, disowned the backgrounder on behalf of the President. That goofy number was the press briefing equivalent of Dunkirk and left Mr. Bushnell lying on the beach while Gen. Haig evacuated.

But this byplay, and the press's predictable reaction to it, should not obscure a more important matter.

The real story is that the administration's propaganda blitz went virtually unchallenged for several weeks. Reacting instinctively, print and broadcast journalists alike initially gave Washington's claims about the El Salvador civil war the kind of over-eager, over-credulous respect which warms the heart of every government flack.

It is hard to understand why, instead of complaining, the State Department didn't hand out commendation medals for outstanding press cooperation. The press play in the opening weeks of the campaign to convince us that El Salvador is the place to roll back the Iron Curtain demonstrated that big government sets the terms of public discussion about major issues far more often than the press likes to admit or the public understands.

How else can the virtually unquestioning press response to the administration's El Salvador white paper be explained? It was swallowed whole and regurgitated in a fashion not equaled since the Johnson administration's white paper on Vietnam 15 years ago.

How else, too, is it possible to explain that for weeks most American press accounts cast the El Salvador conflict in simplistic terms of Communist insurrection against moderate government, with rightist thugs in the wings? Such characterizations flew in the face of the Roman Catholic Church's leading role in opposition to the status quo, the labor movement's courageous efforts to create long-overdue economic changes and the testimony of one diplomatic expert after another that the caricature bore no relationship to reality. Yet the expert witnesses were overshadowed as El Salvador was suddenly discovered to be the focal point of the conflict between East and West.

Playing the story close to the way it was presented by the Reagan team made for dramatic theater. It was theater presaged by earlier press fixation on notions such as "The Castro Connection" to encapsulate revolutionary stirrings in Central America. ("The Repression Connection" or "The Poverty Connection" were apparently not as sexy when it came to televised explanations.) There is a long, if not precisely happy, tradition of similar press behavior in this country, although many in the press business have been busily telling each other that they had learned something from their experiences involving Vietnam and Iran, if not from the Watergate story.

If it weren't for that tradition, the question of what the allegedly massive Communist assistance to the revolutionaries really meant might finally be answered. A tantalizing hint was offered in a quote from an unnamed Pentagon official buried deep in the second of two long articles on the El Salvador situation in the Washington Post. He said that the 200 tons of military equipment the administration says were provided by Communist regimes would be used up by a 200-man company in one week of hard fighting. In other words, the 200 tons of equipment is a molehill instead of a mountain.

Which also could be an absolutely wrong assessment. The point is that the public has no way of knowing, because no one in the mass media has pursued this line of questioning to its conclusion. Too many other similar lines of inquiry were also ignored while the administration set the terms of the national debate on the question of El Salvador.

Many reporters did eventually start asking the hard questions. The record is clear, thanks to Mr. Bushnell, that the administration didn't like the way the story was beginning to develop.

But the administration's reaction, whether Mr. Bushnell's or Mr. Brady's, is largely irrelevant. What is relevant to the American people's ability to decide public issues for themselves is the determination of the press to look quickly below the surface of the official line and to demand clear answers to tough questions at the outset of any such story.

The government—any government—will always try to put the best possible face on its policies. The press has a responsibility to subject each one to rigorous questioning from Day One. It is a responsibility which cannot be met by playing catch up ball six weeks after the government side has opened the game.

September 9, 1982

Some Americans may remember Central America. It is the place in which the dominoes were falling at such a rapid rate early last year [1981] that massive U.S. involvement was required to prevent a Soviet takeover by proxy. That thesis, pounded out on the war drums by then Secretary of State Alexander Haig, so alarmed Congress and the public that there was a sudden cooling off of the public tough talk and a new emphasis on other initiatives.

The changed approach had its desired effect, thanks in part to the media's inherent fickleness. As the hairy-chested rhetoric went out the window, the cameras moved on to the Falklands and the Middle East.

They left too soon. The lowered voices belie Washington's steady raising of the ante. Sure enough, the dominoes are falling, but they are the paper barriers erected by Congress to prevent assistance to regimes whose internal policies breed the revolutions they need our arms to suppress. The administration has changed its tactics, but not its goal, which seems to be to mobilize, direct and use whatever force is necessary to crush rebellion throughout the Caribbean. For the moment, it is willing to use the generals and the generals' civilian front men to do it. When it becomes unavoidably evident that the generals cannot prevail, no matter what the level of our assistance, the way to direct intervention will also have been well prepared.

It is not possible to know the full scale of U.S. involvement in the region, since a significant part of it is clandestine. Last November, the president approved a set of proposals for CIA action, and many of them are presumably under way by now. According to several reports, former members of General Somoza's national guard, along with other mercenaries, are carrying out a full-scale guerrilla war with Nicaragua, striking from bases in Honduras. Given the administration's blind eye to military training exercises by similar forces in Florida, it does not strain logic to suppose they are financed and otherwise supported by agencies of our government.

What is not a matter of conjecture is the fact that there are about the same number of American military advisers in Honduras as in El Salvador, 50 or so in each place, and that the appetite for such help is well whetted. The Honduran defense minister, Col. Jose Serra Hernandez, was recently quoted as saying that "the sending of American troops would be well-seen" by his government. Earlier this summer, Honduran military maneuvers under the direction of U.S. officers were highlighted by the airlift, by U.S. pilots, of 1,000 Honduran soldiers to a town near the Nicaraguan border.

A little over five years ago, Guatemala renounced U.S. military assistance because we criticized its human rights practices. It has been trying to get back on the American dole, and recently its efforts received a public boost from the commander of U.S. military forces in Latin America, Lt. Gen. Wallace H. Nutting, who told a New York Times reporter that it is "imperative" that we resume military assistance to Guatemala. The general is firmly on the reservation, since the president has been trying to persuade Congress to lift restrictions on such aid ever since the March coup in Guatemala.

Most people find little evidence that the human rights situation has been substantially altered for the better there, but that seems irrelevant considering the earlier administration report that El Salvador has made "marred, but real" progress in human rights and therefore remains certifiable for continued assistance. The finding has been contested in many quarters. The moderate acting archbishop in El Salvador, Arturo Rivera y Damas, contended in a recent weekly overview of the country's continuing tragedy that government forces were responsible for most of the 270 political killings reported in El Salvador in the preceding two weeks.

But not even this administration is actually prepared to rest its case for more extensive involvement on the benevolent behavior of its clients. Instead, the thread which ties together its Central American policy is the Moscow-Havana-Managua connection, which is used to justify virtually everything it proposes or intends. Thus a report this month by the State Department, the latest in a long series over the years, outlines what it calls an increasingly close military tie between the Soviet Union and Cuba, notes that Cuba has Latin America's second-largest military force and possesses the capacity to move a "battle-tested . . . force quickly into a combat situation in Central America. . . ." Not coincidentally, administration loyalists in the Senate just marched through a resolution that supported the prevention by any means, "including the force of arms," of the extension of Cuban influence in the Western Hemisphere. Match that with the statement by U.S. Deputy Defense Secretary Nestor Sanchez that "in Honduras, the Cuban-Nicaraguan coalition has been working very hard to prepare the ground-work for an eventual full-scale insurgency . . ." and the outline of what appears to be a carefully constructed rationale for full-blown intervention begins to appear.

Which leaves a question. Does anyone care?

July 28, 1983

It is no longer necessary to read the tea leaves and look for hints in covert CIA activity. The days of posturing rhetoric are over. The United States of America has resurrected gunboat diplomacy and manifest destiny in this hemisphere and intends to pursue both with a gleeful vengeance. In ways incalculably harmful to others and destructive both to our basic interests and our best traditions, the Reagan administration is trying to prove to the world that the New Left was correct, if a little premature, in its critique of America's role in the world: We have become what we profess to oppose.

That, at least, is the message which the president and his cohorts have conveyed over the past few weeks. First, the diplomatic decks were cleared of all those who might be less than totally enthusiastic about the beneficial effects of tidy little wars in the Caribbean. Those now in State Department bureaus and ambassadorial posts are united by two characteristics. They are largely newcomers to the region—its history and its problems—and they are ideologically committed to the proposition that the fate of the United States will be decided on the playing fields of El Salvador, Guatemala, Honduras and Nicaragua. There will be no closet peaceniks in the official ranks when journalists come calling.

Second, a compliant client state, Honduras, was found to serve as the forward base for our activities. From its territory, our subsidized counter-revolutionary army strikes into Nicaragua. Its army is being trained and armed to advance our interests in the name of self-defense. Its brief experiment with democracy is on the way to being destroyed.

Third, Washington abandoned any pretense of caring what the officially sanctioned murderers of El Salvador and Guatemala are doing to their opponents. Come hell or high water, the president has made it clear that he will provide as much of a blank check as Congress will fund for the goons who exercise real control of both countries.

Fourth, the CIA has apparently been handed a bottomless bag of goodies to use in bringing down the Sandinista regime in Nicaragua and, it is not hard to infer, to guarantee the longevity of our stooges elsewhere in the area. Since Nicaragua, despite the real excesses of the Sandinistas, is not spontaneously igniting, we will keep throwing on the gas and lighting the matches until it does. After 50 years without the Marines, Nicaragua will be instructed again in the benefits of hewing to our every desire.

Fifth, those desires have become considerably more expansive than originally stated. Once upon a time, Washington demanded only that Nicaragua stop funneling guns and advisors to the guerillas in El Salvador. Now we say that it must become a democracy, allow free elections and, by implication, blot out all Marxist tendencies. Brezhnev said it no better, if in reverse, to Czechoslovakia. The colonels and the generals of the other Central American nations must find that ardent insistence on democracy at least mildly amusing. They won't blink at the hypocrisy, however, since they expect it of us.

Sixth, so that no one might miss the point, the president has ordered a flotilla into the Caribbean and let it be noised about that its ultimate objective might be a quarantine of Nicaragua, whose 2.5 million inhabitants are portrayed as a clear and present danger to this nation of 230 million and its friends. Presumably, a quarantine would be lifted only after all our conditions, old and new, were accepted.

Finally, the president has brought out that most supple of supple public servants, the morally boneless Henry Kissinger, to head a commission whose only real purpose is to provide the conceptual fig leaf for policy decisions which have already been made. Kissinger will not actually have to bend very much to do his master's bidding on this one, since he has always seen Latin America as a bush league training camp for the big powers' World Series. What is difficult to imagine is what will be left to recommend months hence when the commission issues its report. At the rate events are moving in Central America, at least two regimes will have been toppled and a military solution imposed before Kissinger and Company can issue their rationalizations.

To itemize this wretched progression is almost to trivialize it, because the whole is so much more than the sum of its parts. In the name of fighting the designs of an alien empire, we are behaving like imperialists. In the name of preserving our national security, and therefore presumably our way of life, we are betraying our heritage and making a mockery of our public principles. The work which has been going on behind the closed doors of the National Security Council meetings has been opened to public view, and it looks remarkably like Frankenstein's monster.

Just to prove I'm as tough-minded as the next jingoist, let me quickly add here that we can probably "win" this one. That is, we can impose and police a squalid order in Central America with enough Marines, CIA funding and hired guns. We can create, in short, our own Estonia, Lithuania and Latvia, and be as revered for it—and as secure—as are the Russians with their conquered territories. We will have proved that we're big, tough and mean—like any other bully ten times bigger than its victim—and that we intend to be permanent senior partners in a system which relegates the vast majority of all Central Americans to grinding poverty and repression. That may make some of my fellow Americans feel good about their country again. It ought to make all of us feel sick.

April 12, 1984

The question, finally, is whether anyone really cares that this nation's tattered vestiges of moral authority are being systematically stripped away by an administration whose schoolyard bully's approach to the world is a disgrace to our ideals and a boon to our enemies.

There are no fig leafs left for Congress or the public to hide behind. With its open involvement in the mining of Nicaragua's harbors, the Reagan administration has served public notice that it holds international law and congressional intent in contempt. With its refusal to participate in the deliberations of the World Court, a court this nation used to its own advantage as recently as the late 1970s, Washington has joined the polecat nations it so regularly excoriates. We have become the Iran of the 1980s, holding Nicaragua hostage to our obsession with the "great Satan," communism, and in the name of that obsession there is nothing we seem unwilling to do.

This government's foreign enemies have never been in doubt about what it was doing. The deception and doubletalk have been aimed at the American people, who have been treated to endless sermons about the duplicity of our "godless" adversaries and assurances of our place as "a shining city set on a hill." And because some of the people seemed to buy the hypocrisy and to applaud our use of methods we fervently condemn when employed by others, while still others seemed unmoved by each new revelation, Congress has for the most part rolled over and played dead.

Consider the irony of the repeated attacks last week by the president, his secretary of state and other spokesmen on congressional "interference" with the implementation of an effective foreign policy.

During that week, and before the public revelation of the Central Intelligence Agency's hit-and-run mining games in Nicaraguan waters, the Senate supinely approved yet more money for the CIA's "covert" activities against Nicaragua. And while the president was flaying congressional Democrats for allegedly causing the failure of his military adventure in Lebanon, he was actually highlighting the stark reality that Congress, in that instance as in all others over the past three years, has not blocked one significant iota of policy. Indeed, whether the subject was troops in Lebanon or military aid to Central America, MX missiles in vulnerable Minuteman silos or the invasion of a tiny island state, huffing and puffing on Capitol Hill has been followed inevitably by acquiescence to the substance, if not the form, of what the president proposed.

What the president has been doing to and around Nicaragua is quite clearly, as Sen. Barry Goldwater reportedly put it in a letter this week to CIA Director William Casey, an "act of war." It is also terrorism, as defined by the president and both of his secretaries of state. As surely as a bomb planted on a bus will kill innocent nonbelligerents, a U.S.-financed terrorist who slits a civilian throat in the north of Nicaragua is no less a terrorist than the Khomeini-worshiping fanatic who rams a dynamite-laden truck into an embassy compound or Marine headquarters. Both are the fruits of "state terrorism."

And that is why the U.S. was isolated in the Security Council vote condemning the mining of Nicaraguan waters and why the British and French have been publicly explicit in their opposition to what we have been doing. It is why we find ourselves viewed from afar not as the "shining city" of the president's inaugural address, but as an enraged bull that is intent on rending and goring all those with whom it disagrees. With far greater effect than anything our adversaries have contrived, our government is inflicting ever more severe wounds on the U.S. itself in the name of the national interest.

The president, when he is not accusing the Democrats of responsibility for each of his multiple failures abroad, has taken to demanding a return to bipartisanship in foreign policy. It's a good idea. Republicans and Democrats alike, for the sake of the Constitution as well as international agreements and law, should unite to bring a runaway, lunatic and ultimately destructive foreign policy under control. They should require an end to undeclared war against the integrity of another state. They should take the weapons from the hands of those whose chief victims are civilians of every age and both sexes.

All that is required is enough courage to withstand the demagoguery that equates adherence to principle with "softness" and claims there can be no solution to any international problem without the use of the unsheathed sword. All that is required is the willingness to talk sense to the people, to tell them that nothing is gained and all is lost by aping the tactics of those we most despise.

If Congress could actually muster that kind of courage, not only as it relates to Central America but to the world at large, we would take a long step toward refashioning a truly bipartisan foreign-policy consensus that could command majority support. Without it, all that is left is the law of the jungle, in which we do unto others as they do unto us until not one of us is left standing. But do enough Americans, politicians or private citizens, really care enough to begin the process where and when it matters—right here and right now? We shall soon see.

October 25, 1984

Sometimes it's hard to believe that this isn't 1975. The revelations about the activities of our paid terrorists in and around Nicaragua sound like a replay of the stories that unfolded before Congress a decade ago, stories that confirmed the CIA had behaved abroad in ways more popularly ascribed to the KGB—and that it had done so with the knowledge, consent or direction of the White House. Congressional oversight was supposed to cure all that, but it hasn't, and it's time for the public and politicians alike to take yet another hard look at the actions and accountability of an agency whose chief function is supposedly contained in its name.

In the brave new world of 1984, words mean what government officials say they mean, as former CIA chief George Bush has been demonstrating lately. Nonetheless, "intelligence," as in the second word in the CIA's title, is said by my dictionary to mean: "(1) mental ability, the power of learning and understanding; (2) information, news, especially that of military value; (3) the people engaged in collecting this."

What does any of this have to do with the mining of harbors of a nation with which we are not at war, the financing of random murder of civilians as well as government officials and the instruction of former Somoza thugs in whatever techniques of terrorism our money did not help them learn during their murderous reign in Managua?

As we are often told, however, we must not be naive. This is a tough world in which real enemies plot real threats to the national interest. If we are to be forewarned and therefore forearmed, we must have a first-rate intelligence agency—and that includes a first-rate espionage capacity. (As my dictionary sees it, espionage means "spying or using spies to obtain secret information.")

All but a few of us would concede, grudgingly or not, that spying and human history go hand in hand and that so-called "human intelligence" remains vitally important in the deadly world we inhabit. But what does that have to do with a manual that teaches our clients how to "neutralize" public officials "such as court judges, police and state security officials. Gather together the population affected so that they will be present and take part in the act . . ."? That's not spying and that isn't intelligence. That's murder.

At this point in the discussion, apologists for such activity tend to lower their voices and speak firmly of the need to fight fire with fire. It is the nature of Communist regimes, we are told, to do such things, and they must never forget that two can tango. But we are not a totalitarian police state and our ideology carries no justification for putting ends above means. Play the ape long enough and you become an ape, which stands both creationism and evolution on their heads but which accurately reflects the way things happen in human society.

And that is the point of what we have been doing in Central America, if not elsewhere. The CIA, given what was apparently extraordinary latitude by a presidential directive in late 1981, has simply cast off its new restrictions and gone back to the bad old days with a vengeance. For any who doubt it, we have the word of the president himself, who confirmed in the Sunday night debate, that agency employees are indeed hard at work in Central America and have been directly involved with the terrorism manual and other good deeds. (As an old government spokesman who was always instructed to offer a stiff "no comment" when asked about intelligence activities, I fell back in amused shock when the president publicly confirmed all but the details of the agency's role in the region. The only aspect of his remarks more ludicrous than the fact that he uttered them at all was his retraction of the apparent admission that CIA operatives are in Nicaragua itself. Of course they are.)

But, so too, are they in El Salvador, dying in plane crashes while trying to intercept those extraordinarily elusive "massive arms shipments" from Nicaragua about which we keep hearing so much but seeing so little. So too are they in Costa Rica and Honduras in great numbers. In the latter nation, they are publicly gathered in ways that already parody their presence in Vietnam 15 years ago.

How much of this has been authorized by Congress? To hear

those responsible for congressional oversight, including such men as Barry Goldwater and Daniel Patrick Moynihan, almost none. Each new revelation provokes expressions of congressional outrage or cautious disapproval. Occasionally, new restrictions are voted and promptly ignored. How much of it had and has the approval, explicit or implicit, of the president? To hear him tell it, almost none. But if Congress and the president have not approved U.S.-financed war and U.S.-financed terrorism, then the CIA is out of control, and the question arises: Who is in charge here, a secret organ of state security or the state?

Finally, one other word that was briefly surfaced and then "newspeaked" to death by the vice president. The word is shame. As my dictionary sees it, the preferred definition is: "A painful mental feeling aroused by a sense of having done something wrong or dishonorable or improper or ridiculous." It's the right word for the moment, and it will take more than White House double-talk to expunge it.

21

The Sleight of Hand in Lebanon

October 6, 1983

Back in April, one of my columns supporting the Marines' peacekeeping role in Lebanon brought a deluge of outraged dissent. "This is crazy," wrote one gentleman. These days, I find myself echoing his remark, although in a somewhat different context. What seems crazy is not that the U.S. remains involved in the search for stability in Lebanon, but that the administration continues to change the rules of the game and its objectives while denying there has been any real change and refusing to share its thinking with the American people.

This has nothing to do with the struggle over invocation of the War Powers Resolution of 1973, a struggle apparently resolved by a fig leaf compromise which satisfies no one and evades the basic constitutional issue, though the deal is probably the best that could be expected. The president will get congressional backing for a long-term stay in Lebanon by the Marine contingent already there, if the agreement holds, and Congress gains presidential acknowledgment that the resolution exists. There will be no showdown, no test of the resolution's real meaning, but that may be for the best in the immediate situation.

What is not for the best is further postponement of a full explanation of exactly what Washington sees as our role in Lebanon today and a full-scale debate in Congress of that policy. We have come a very long distance in a very short time from the decision in September 1982, to send in the Marines to help "to restore Lebanese government sovereignty and authority over the Beirut area" following the refugee camp massacres. At that time, the president explicitly stated "there is no intention nor expectation that U.S. armed forces will become involved in hostilities."

A little less than a year later, the Marines were involved in such hostilities, four men had died and several dozen had been wounded. The Lebanese government, increasingly run by and for the Christian minority in Lebanon, was fighting with a broad variety of sectarian and foreign enemies, and Washington now seemed to see its mission as the preservation of the government and its army.

That is not precisely the way that administration and military spokesmen are putting it, but that is what American shelling of anti-government positions in the mountains outside Beirut actually means. White House press secretary Larry Speakes offered the new official line on Monday, declaring that: "The successful Lebanese Army force defense of the area is vital to the safety of U.S. personnel, including the U.S. multinational force, other U.S. military and the U.S. diplomatic corps presence. If hostile force should take the high ground . . . , they would pose a threat to the safety of our international contingent." Unfortunately, "hostile" forces located in a number of other areas near and around Marine positions near the Beirut airport already posed a threat "to the safety of our international contingent." If the success of the Lebanese Army is central to such safety, we have become full participants in the fighting, willy-nilly. Thus Marine and U.S. Army personnel are on the front lines with the Lebanese Army in the mountains as "observers." Thus American ships are blasting away at Druse, Palestinean and Syrian positions. Thus American air power seems poised to participate in the battles to come.

All of this is another way of saying that we are at war in fact if not in name, and the logic of what we are doing is that we will have to become more involved in the near future if our present policy is to bear fruit. But just how involved? To what achievable purpose? With what long-range hopes and short-range objectives?

What we are witnessing is involvement by incrementalism, which substitutes motion for policy and sleight of hand for informed consent by the American people. It's the wrong way to approach an admittedly complicated task. Instead, to repeat something I also wrote last April, "the president would be well-advised to go to Congress with a full-dress proposal for a continued U.S. military presence . . . What we intend to do . . . should be fully understood and fully approved in advance. Having that approval, the president will be far more able to convince others in the region that we are serious about our long-term commitment to Lebanon's future stability and development."

If there is no comprehensive proposal in hand, if we are substituting ad hoc reaction for policy, then we should be planning for withdrawal at the earliest possible time. If there is a policy, it should be shared promptly with Congress and the public. We still have a vital role to play in Lebanon, but it is a role which must be understood and endorsed by the country at large if it is to have a chance of success.

December 22, 1983

The president spent much of his press conference this week, justifying, explaining and defending the American military role in Lebanon. He had good reason. Domestic opposition to our apparently open-ended mission there has been growing rapidly, cutting across the ideological spectrum and including many who once supported the deployment of Marines to Beirut.

But while he was asked repeatedly, and responded repeatedly, about American intentions in Lebanon, he touched only once, and then indirectly, on a more fundamental issue for which Lebanon is simply the most current metaphor. That issue is the new definition of war, a state of being that for post-World War II America has become as seemingly endless as it has become extraordinarily imprecise.

By almost any standard of American history, the Marines stationed in Lebanon, along with the associated Navy and Army personnel, are in combat. Lives have been lost by the hundreds. The battleship New Jersey's largest guns have been turned on the "enemy" in the hills outside Beirut. American planes have been downed by Syrian missiles and American planes have pounded Syrian and other positions.

But in response to a question as to whether he considered Lt. Robert Goodman, the downed American airman, a hostage, President Reagan replied in part: "The Syrians claim that he is a prisoner of war. Well, I don't know how you have a prisoner of war when there is no declared war between nations."

Which leads directly to the main point, which is easy to forget but startling when considered. The U.S. has lost more than 100,000 servicemen in battle since 1945, but Congress has not declared war since December 1941. In the intervening years, our troops have heard weapons fired in anger from Latin America to Southeast Asia to the Middle East, and have been placed in potentially explosive situations more times than most people can easily count. We have run warlike maneuvers, with military as well as political purpose, in the Caribbean, the Mediterranean, the North Atlantic and the Pacific, among other bodies of water, and have sent our planes without permission across the airspace of unfriendly nations repeatedly.

What is more, Americans acting in their official capacity have helped with, fomented or been active participants in wars ranging from the jungles of Angola to the bush of Nicaragua. The CIA, at presidential direction or with presidential complicity, repeatedly attempted the assassination of at least one leader of a foreign country with which we were not at war, bought insurrection in innumerable nations and subsidized the political opposition to both legitimate and illegitimate regimes around the world. All, by normal definition, were acts of war.

The euphemisms employed to blur the reality that a war is a war have been as ingenious as they have been disingenuous. There have been "police actions" and "rescue missions." We have fought to save others from aggression and to preserve democracy. Washington has acted at the mandate of the United Nations and in opposition to its resolutions. We have united for peace and moved unilaterally.

Our government has, in short, adopted whatever approach seemed most expedient at the time, but never the one that the Constitution would seem to require. Congress has not been asked to declare war nor demanded through its power of the purse that warlike activity cease until it did so. When it comes to the new world of the endless Cold War and its attendant hot-war engagements, the Constitution is a dead letter.

With that as a background, the War Powers Act, rather than being the impediment to executive action that several presidents have decried, should be seen as what it is, implicit congressional endorsement of presidential war-making. It has yet to be used in a way that would promptly remove America from an undeclared war, it has been ignored by one White House after another during the critical period of initial involvement in combat and it has largely served as an after-the-fact vehicle for Congress to give assent to actions it lacked the will to oppose in meaningful ways when it mattered.

What exists in fact rather than theory for the U.S. in the latter half of the 20th century is a permanent state of war marked by regular outbreaks of sustained fighting and occasional uneasy cease-fires. It is a condition into which we have moved imperceptibly but inexorably. It is the garrison state, in which the constitutional constraints of an earlier age are regarded too often as meaningless if not dangerous obstacles to tough-minded pursuit of national interests and national security.

Perhaps that is as the people want it, but they should at least be given the opportunity to vote yes or no. If congressional war-making is now a dead letter, let the Constitution be amended to reflect it, so that at least we can maintain the pretense that we live in a nation governed by law. If the clutch of men running for the presidency and the man who now occupies that post are all agreed that there is no alternative to this condition, then let them say so. But if there is even one person seeking the White House who disagrees, the long campaign is the time to raise the issue, publicly and repeatedly. We have come a very long way down the road that leads to total unrestrained executive power to commit this nation to war, but the journey is not yet over. It's past time an effort was made to reverse course.

January 5, 1984

"Responsibility, yes; culpability, no."

That was the memorable attempt of a well-known, if ostensibly anonymous, White House source to explain why no one should finally be held accountable for the Beirut disaster.

It is a definitional distinction without a difference, and no phrase better summarizes the president's scrambling effort to deflect public opinion from the central thrust of the congressional and Defense Department reports on the calamity.

Reading between the lines of the New York Times story that quoted the high administration official, one is forced to the conclusion that the person in question must come from the ranks of those who learned their trade in the Nixon White House.

Only one so schooled could have such contempt for the good sense of the people, such a low regard for their ability to pick up a dictionary if necessary to see whether there really is, as the source put it, a difference between responsibility and culpability.

There isn't. One who is culpable deserves blame. One who is responsible is "legally or morally obliged to take care of something or to carry out a duty; liable to be blamed for a loss or failure," according to the Oxford American Dictionary.

And as both the House subcommittee report and the five-man Defense Department investigation made clear, there is plenty of blame to go around, starting at the top and going down to the front lines in Lebanon.

In an extraordinarily cynical attempt at pre-emption, the president last week tried to subsume all discussion in one sweeping, morally hazy assumption of total responsibility for a limited area of accountability.

It was hazy by design. The key statement begins, "If there is to be blame." Not, "As two reports have made clear, there is blame." Not, "My own Defense Department has now underscored the places where blame should be placed."

No, that disingenuous bit of fluff, "If there is to be blame, it properly rests here in this office and with this president. And I accept responsibility for the bad as well as the good."

Politically and constitutionally, the president was stating a simple truth—once you got past the disclaimer at the top of the remark. The conduct of any administration is ultimately the responsibility of the president, abroad as well as at home. But as the Defense Department report observed:

"The commission holds the view that military commanders are responsible for the performance of their subordinates. The commander can delegate some or all of his authority to his subordinates, but he cannot delegate his responsibility for the performance of the forces he commands."

This was the view the president rejected in what amounted to a blanket pardon. It prompted a question from one former high-ranking officer:

"If the system isn't given a chance to establish accountability, how can you expect officers to fear the results of failure?"

But it was not consideration for the careers and sensibilities of the responsible field commanders that prompted the hasty presidential pre-emption. It was the immediate recognition at the White House that the commission's report said a great deal more about responsibility (or culpability) for the Oct. 23 horror in Beirut than the failure of military commanders to take adequate measures for the security of their personnel.

In dry-as-dust language, the indictment rolls out. What was envisioned as a peace-keeping mission at the beginning, to operate in a relatively benign, studiously neutral environment, became instead a partisan mission, operating in a hostile environment to support one of the participants in a bitter civil war. All of this "effectively precluded the possibility of a successful peacekeeping mission. . . . The commission believes that appropriate guidance . . . should have been provided . . . to enable (the American force) to cope effectively with the increasingly hostile environment. The commission could find no evidence that such guidance was, in fact, provided."

In other words, the Marines on the ground became hostage to

and ultimately victims of a policy that bore no relationship to reality.

In the wake of the mass murder of the bivouacked Marines, the commission cites an "urgent need for reassessment of alternate means to achieve U.S. objectives in Lebanon . . . and a more vigorous and demanding approach to pursuing diplomatic alternatives."

Small wonder that a president who was making the grand gesture of personal responsibility was also ensuring that most Americans would never be able to see the report. No copies were initially made available to the public. A grand total of 200 were issued on Dec. 28, with 100 going to the press and 100 to Congress, the armed forces and other institutional groups.

Responsibility, yes; culpability, yes. The Defense Department commission made the unbreakable connection between presidential policy and American tragedy. All the obfuscation, moral myopia and public relations fuzz in the world cannot break it.

31

The Iran–Contra Affair: "A Separate Morality"

December 4, 1986

"We gave you the staff to help you direct the other departments, not to evade or undermine them, not to roam about the world setting off wars, revolutions, panic, pandemonium and, most emphatically and fundamentally, Mr. President, not to break the laws Congress has enacted."

The subject was the National Security Council staff, the speaker was Sen. Daniel Patrick Moynihan (D., N.Y.) and, allowing for hyperbole, the words went to the nub of the scandal that has shaken the Reagan presidency. If you want to understand the Amazing Comics capers involving the NSC, Iran, Israel, the contras and a potential cast of thousands, look no further. And if Congress wants them to recur in the not-distant future, all it has to do is fail to change fundamentally the rules that govern the NSC staff and director.

But if the NSC's private foreign policy (or at least, seemingly private) can best be explained by allusions to loose cannons, there is a deeper explanation for why those who played fast and loose with their power acted as they did. It was foreshadowed by something Hugh Sloan, treasurer of the Nixon reelection committee in 1972, said before he resigned. He described the atmosphere in the Nixon administration during Watergate by saying: "There was no independent sense of morality there. I mean, if you worked for someone, he was God and whatever the orders were, you did it—and there were damned few who were able or willing to make independent judgments. . . . It was all so narrow, so closed. . . . There emerged some kind of separate morality about things."

It is that "separate morality" we have been smelling around Washington for six years. The ideological truth, as promulgated by a president whose "truths" are rarely disturbed by facts, has been used to justify almost anything. For the true believers who were placed in positions of influence and power, their mission was so holy that nothing should be allowed to stand in its way—not laws, not public opinion, not court orders and not Congress.

Did everyone else, and all previous presidents, understand the clear demands of court rulings and legislative acts in the field of civil rights? Too bad. It was time to subvert them. Did the courts demand certain behavior in the distribution of disability benefits?

Ignore the courts. Did everyone involved with the negotiation of the Anti-Ballistic Missile Treaty say that it was clearly meant to forbid certain forms of development and deployment? Simply contradict them and violate the treaty as you see fit. Did Congress intend that the Superfund be implemented with evenhanded firmness? To hell with Congress.

A "separate morality about things": Thus Lt. Col. Oliver North, the man held out to us as the sole architect of the Iran-Contra connection, is explained by his former associate, Michael Ledeen, as one who did nothing "that didn't reflect the convictions of his superiors." As for Congress, its laws and the media, the colonel is repeatedly described as holding them all in contempt. On the one side, revealed truth; on the other, the checks and balances of a democratic republic of divided authority.

In this administration, Lt. Col. North is no exception. Even as he was revealing the evidence of diversion of funds to the contras, Attorney General Edwin Meese was demanding unswerving loyalty from the president's team. In Washington today, no trespass of legal responsibility is considered an adequate ground for resignation or sustained opposition. Secretary of State George Shultz went out and played the good soldier, if not the good German. "I think the president has been giving magnificent leadership. . . . I am proud to be a part of the president's efforts in this regard."

Finally, there was White House counsel Peter J. Wallison. Asked by the New York Times whether the administration upheld the laws it disliked or simply ignored them, he replied: "I'm not going to be able to say anything. I just have no comment on that." There, at least, honesty compelled silence.

"There is a bitter bile in my throat," the president told his sycophantic Time magazine interviewer, Hugh Sidey. In *his* throat? Surely he was jesting, or attempting to describe the way millions of his once-loyal public now feel. This from the president who had once proclaimed that "America will never make concessions to terrorists," and then made them. This from a president who was forced to fire Lt. Col. North, and who then hailed him as a "national hero." What would he have called Gordon Liddy of Watergate?

It is now up to Congress, the special prosecutor and the press to probe deeply into the question of how wide the net of complicity and blame should be cast. More than one of our contemporary Holy Crusaders will have to face the consequences of forgetting that ours is supposed to be a government of laws and not men.

But the law itself must be changed so that the National Security Council structure is no longer such a convenient spot to lodge activities forbidden by law or public policy. All operations must be explicitly forbidden to the NSC staff and director, with appropriate criminal penalties for violations. If the NSC director is not to be made subject to confirmation, as the Senate would have required seven years ago, then he must be forcefully confined to the role of adviser and traffic cop. Otherwise, sooner rather than later other men will be found who are willing to play by the rules of a "separate morality," and yet another administration will be shaken to its foundations and the country with it.

January 29, 1987

The president spent not quite 250 words Tuesday, defending, explaining and then waving away his Iranian arms sale disaster. Partisanship over a "worthy" policy that "did not work," in which "serious mistakes were made," must not be allowed to weaken us, he said. In any case, "we will not sit idly by if our interests or our friends in the Middle East are threatened, nor will we yield to terrorist blackmail."

In his own words, Mr. Reagan once more revealed that he either doesn't understand the full consequences of his fatally flawed exercise in Realpolitik or else believes the public can be faked into believing nothing of real importance has happened. It's not a palatable set of alternatives.

To understand just how badly the policy went wrong and how grave have been its results, consider first what was involved. The weapons we provided to Iran were not "peanuts," Secretary of State George Shultz's testimony to Congress this week notwithstanding. There are military experts who believe they have helped tip the balance in the recent fighting between Iran and Iraq. But the significant weapons transfers have been made over several years by Israel—and those were made with the consent and support of the president and his men. Other weapons were sold directly by such allies as Portugal.

None could have made it to Tehran without American knowledge. All went directly to sustain the Iranian war machine at a time when Washington's official, public policy was to prevent any nation or private supplier from making weapons available to that same machine. Given what is now known about the hidden reality of the past several years, who is suppose to take us seriously? The U.S. is demonstrably either hypocritical or impotent, or both. The ayatollah's men portray the president as a groveling petitioner, a paper tiger and a false friend, and they are bound to have a receptive audience.

That is the critical point. There has been one clear winner as a result of the president's "serious mistakes," and it is Iran. There has been one clear loser, and it is the U.S. The second point is the one that even now the president cannot bring himself to make. It is not just that "full responsibility" for the fiasco is his. That almost literally should go without saying, since he is the president. What matters is that the "serious mistakes" were primarily his.

As a result of them, we are now deploying the Navy to the area to reassure our allies. It's too late. The revelations of our duplicitous dealings have strengthened Iran's political as well as military position. Rather than being the target of great power pressure, Iran is now seen as the beneficiary of great power largesse, with the Great Satan itself in the forefront of the gift givers. Each time the president or one of his spokesmen repeats anew the assertion that our long-term interests in the Mideast will be served by a closer relationship to Tehran, our client states along the Persian Gulf shiver. They no longer have to suspect that we will throw them, and Iraq, over the minute that Tehran gives the right signal. They know we have already done so.

There is a phrase much in favor among diplomacy buffs. We "play the China card," or whatever, in relation to a competition with a third nation. In Tehran, the mullahs have been immeasurably strengthened in yet another way by the sure knowledge that they can always play the "American card." That knowledge is aimed squarely at the Soviets. It's just as well it exists, but it adds considerably to the stability of the ayatollah's regime.

On yet another front, Iran emerges the clear winner. Because, as the president put it, we were willing to pay ransom "to try to secure freedom for our citizens held in barbaric captivity," no one can officially admit the obvious, which is that the payment was a signal to hostage-takers that much could be gained by adding to their stock and little would be risked.

Because of the convoluted exercises necessary to distance the president from the rash of new seizures that have occurred in recent months, the fiction that Iran has no connection with them must be maintained. And since Iran is repeatedly absolved of responsibility, its agents need not fear that their patron will be harmed. That is the reality against which the president's pledge that "we will not sit idly by" nor "yield to terrorist blackmail" must be measured. We do and we have, and everyone in the Middle East knows it.

There is much to be done as "we go forward together in the national interest," as the president would have us do. A new anti-terrorism policy must be manufactured from the rubble of the old one. A prolonged period of confidence-building lies ahead with Jordan, Saudi Arabia, Iraq, the Persian Gulf states and others. Iran must be constrained from using the muscles we have provided to pound the area into hegemonic conformity.

The president warned that "in debating the past, we must not deny ourselves the successes of the future." But until there is full understanding of what the failures of the past have produced, there is no way to build anything approximating success in the future. Given the president's absolute refusal to participate in that exercise, it is up to Congress, on both sides of the aisle, to continue to work on the problem.

March 12, 1987

After near-record snowfalls, a false spring came to Washington earlier this month. The crocuses popped up, buds plumped out to the explosion point and the kids came out by the thousands in shorts and halter tops. The optimistic illusion was shattered Sunday night when a light dusting of snow accompanied a sharp drop in the temperature. The heavy coats came back out again and everyone was reminded that it wasn't smart to mess around with Mother Nature. Winter, like a ball game, ain't over till it's over.

That's not a bad analogy for the state of affairs in Washington today, and at the White House in particular. After a heavy winter of political discontent, the president managed to produce his own false spring with a shrewdly conceived and superbly executed speech in which he slipped neatly around a real explanation while accepting responsibility for those things for which his office obviously made him responsible. The speech was accompanied by some notable comings and goings in high executive branch offices.

At the end, the glow of Howard Baker's obvious competence and William Webster's incandescent integrity warmed the hearts of all but the unreconstructed warriors of the far right. There was a noticeable revival of belief, or hope, that the president had come through the bad days almost unscathed.

It's a possible outcome, but at present a premature conclusion. Unlike the rites of spring, there is no predestination involved. And as the days have marched by after The Speech and the Baker-Webster appointments, the chill winds of political reality have begun to blow again.

Their source can be found in two places. First, there is public opinion, a notoriously fickle force but a significant factor in the success of the Reagan presidency. All the instant polls showed an instant revival of the president's popularity, though not as dramatic as loyalists had hoped for. But the follow-up focus-group discussions, whether more or less scientific, left a different impression. A lot of people still like the president, but many fewer now trust him. "Arms to the terrorists" is not a popular slogan; nor are presidential lies, even in a good cause, acceptable to most of the voters.

Second, the practicing politicians of both parties are far more downbeat, if not downright cynical, in their private forecasts about the administration's future vitality than they are in public. To hear most of them talk, this is an impotent presidency, even if some of its major ideas survive. "Brain damaged" is a phrase much uttered in connection with its sense of direction and power of purpose. Again, it is a phrase whose utterance leaps party lines and ideological labels. As many see it, Howard Baker can keep the White House from hitting any more shoals but is powerless to restore full power ahead.

It would be wrong to attribute this perception entirely to the consequences of the Iran-Contra scandal. Drift and missteps were there for all to see for months before the revelations of November. Nor can the gift from Mikhail Gorbachev in the form of the administration's own intermediate-missile zero-option proposal do much to affect this perception where and when it matters most. By the time a deal is struck, if indeed the bombs-away hard-liners among the civilians at the Pentagon and at the Arms Control and Disarmament Agency are unable to block it, the president will be a lame duck in fact as well as Democratic wish. Everyone and his brother (or sister) will be out running for election to his office, and the office will be diminished accordingly.

What looms over everything, however, are the unanswered questions about the diverted Iranian arms money. Linked to those questions is the persistently unpopular administration obsession with the war against the Sandinistas. The Contras, as we were reminded by the New York Times once more on Tuesday, continue to behave like terrorists in the field, murdering civilians with a zeal they rarely apply to pitched battles with the Sandinista military units.

As for their democratic intentions, they were called into question once more when their Hamlet-in-residence, Arturo Cruz, announced his final and definitive resignation from all association with them. Mr. Cruz is many things, but most important of all, he has been the State Department's fig leaf of democratic good faith, disguising by his presence the essentially undemocratic tendencies of most of the other "Founding Fathers" and "freedom fighters." With him gone, few will mourn whatever the congressional committees, special prosecutors and grand juries uncover.

And that is the final point. There are months of dirty revelations yet to come. Every delaying tactic, such as Oliver North's attempt to gut the special prosecutor, only prolongs the ordeal.

And while no one revelation will be fatal and many may eventually come to seem boringly old hat, death can come by a thousand cuts as surely as from a swift beheading.

Real spring, in short, is still far off for the Reagan presidency. Assuming it does finally arrive, the odds are that most people will be too involved in the selection of the new ruler to care either way how it all came out for the old one.

May 14, 1987

Robert C. McFarlane, the former national security adviser, went to the nub of the matter in his opening statement at the congressional hearings on Monday. It is hard to improve on his indictment of the fundamental flaw in the administration's approach both to arms dealings with Iran and to secret support of the Contras in Central America. As he said, having stressed that he and the president felt strongly that defeat of Soviet ambitions in Nicaragua was essential in order to deter Soviet designs elsewhere in the world:

"We had to win this one. And this is where the administration made its first mistake. For if we had such a large strategic stake, it was clearly unwise to rely on covert activity as the core of our policy. . . . You must have the American people and the U.S. Congress solidly behind you. Yet it is virtually impossible, almost as a matter of definition, to rally public support behind a policy that you can't even talk about."

And there you have it. The president and his men, from buccaneer patriots like retired Maj. Gen. Richard Secord to stolid veterans of the national security apparatus like Bud McFarlane, simply ignored the fact that they live in a nation in which the informed consent of the governed is the presumed first requirement of public policy. All else flowed from that: the lies, the law-breaking, the Swiss bank accounts, the privateer warriors, the privatization of foreign policy, the destruction of presidential prestige. Having been unable to "rally public support" behind one policy—aid to the Contras—and having pledged never to pursue another—aid to terrorists—the president and his men proceeded to act in secret in ways they could not act in public.

It was and is profoundly anti-democratic, but the ease with which it was all accomplished and the administration's sustained ability to keep it hidden from the American people reveal how dangerously far we have moved from the requirement of political accountability. The apparatus of the national security state was fully utilized to support policies the democratic polity had not endorsed—and not a single administration official who knew what was happening had the decency and moral courage to stand up in public and oppose it. Not anyone in the National Security Council, not the vice president, not the secretary of state, not the secretary of defense, not a clutch of assistant secretaries and their minions and most definitely not the late CIA director, William Casey.

Some, like Mr. Casey and his agency, were ardent supporters and in it up to their eyeballs. Some, like Secretary of State George Shultz, were actively involved in part of it and opposed to part. But all either kept quiet or encouraged their subordinates in embassies and military bases around the world to go along.

Pontius Pilate or active conspirator, none measured up to his responsibility to the nation.

Watching both Gen. Secord and Mr. McFarlane, I was reminded of the old West Point motto of "Duty, Honor, Country." It is a creed worth emblazoning on every mantle, so long as it is properly understood. But "country" is not synonymous with either president or government. "Duty" properly defined is not to orders from the chain of command but to the imperatives of constitutional government. And "honor" lies in measuring up to a moral code larger than current policy.

Gen. Secord, speaking of his co-conspirators in the grand game of aid-the-Contras, Lt. Col. Oliver North and Vice Adm. John Poindexter, said, "They are both dedicated and honest men who in my view tried diligently and conscientiously to carry out the policies of the president in an appropriate manner." And so they must all have seemed to each other, living in that closed world of certitude in which their patriotism and their leader's sensible policies seem unfairly hemmed in by the restrictions and harassment of Congress, press and public. They would not and could not accept the constitutional truth expressed by Sen. Daniel Inouye that "the president may be the senior partner in foreign policy, but he is not the sole proprietor."

It was somehow appropriate that Gary Hart's self-destruction coincided with Gen. Secord's testimony. Both men believe themselves to be people whose devotion to the nation's future is above reproach. Both believe that they have been unfairly persecuted for reasons that are irrelevant to the larger issues with which they were engaged. Both are incapable of admitting that there was anything fundamentally wrong with what they did in secret, since their public motives were, by their own lights, so pure.

But in the case of both Gary Hart and Richard Secord (and

all those who were engaged in one aspect or another of the larger "enterprise" to which Gen. Secord was attached), what was conducted "off the books" went off the tracks as well. "Out of sight and out of control" could well be the epitaph for both. But what was no more than personal self-destruction for Mr. Hart, sad as that was, has far more dangerous implications for the nation in the case of the president and his loyal men. It is not just "folly and hypocrisy," as Sen. William Cohen termed the Iranian arms deal. It is a radical assault on the underlying principles of this democratic republic, none more important than the stricture that government cannot do behind closed doors what the people would not approve when they are open.

July 16, 1987

Years ago, one of the veterans of radio soap opera who had made a successful transition to television was asked how he managed to keep grinding out his three-handkerchief performances day after day. "It's easy," he replied. "Once you learn to fake sincerity, you've got it licked."

His words have surfaced repeatedly in my memory as the Iran-Contra conspiracy has come unraveled in public view, but never so often as during Lt. Col. Oliver North's six-day virtuoso performance. The man could play any part in the repertoire, with the possible exception of Quasimodo, and do equally well.

The problem, however, is that the colonel's testimony, stripped of peroration and hyperbole, boils down to an itemized rebuttal of the sworn and unsworn recollections of virtually the entire national security hierarchy. If the colonel is telling the truth, an extraordinary range of other public officials has been lying.

Even as Rear Adm. John Poindexter endures his moment in the spotlight, adding his sincerity to the general stew, the point-by-point contradictions between the claims of Col. North and his former boss, Robert McFarlane, loom in the background like Banquo's ghost. Those points of contention illustrate the larger problems facing the president and his men.

Mr. McFarlane and Col. North disagree on whether Mr. McFarlane ordered Col. North to alter documents. They also disagree on whether the Boland amendment applied to the National Security Council. The one-time NSC chief says that, contrary to Col. North's words, he was not kept informed of all of his aide's activities. Mr. McFarlane says he did not give prior approval to the use of retired Gen. Richard Secord in establishing a covert arms network for the Contras. And, finally, he does not recall any plan to make Col. North the fall guy if the secret operations were disclosed.

Some of this is petty and some of it is significant. Whatever it is, it is only the tip of an iceberg of clashing recollections and downright lies.

All the witnesses appear to have gone to school with the greatest star of them all, the president of the United States. His has been the model in more ways than one right from the start. It was President Reagan, after all, who said:

"We did not—repeat, did not—trade weapons or anything else for hostages, nor will we."

Speculation about secret arms dealings with Iran "has no foundation."

"We . . . have had nothing to do with other countries or their shipment of arms or doing what they're doing."

"Yes," the secretaries of state and defense supported the Iranian arms sale. "We have all been working together."

One of the whoppers was retracted within an hour, one within a week and one after four months. All the retractions were grudging concessions to truth, wrung from the old trouper by facts that could not be shoved aside. And each admission was offered up with that air of frank, open-faced sincerity that has been the president's stock-in-trade for all of his public life.

On the basis of these two weeks in July, Oliver North is arguably the president's logical successor as public thespian, though not, let us pray, as president. But there are many other aspirants, almost all of whom will have been heard from before the congressional hearings are over. William Casey, the late head of the CIA, no longer qualifies. But as with all the rest, Col. North's words are damning. The colonel claims that his mentor was in on the diversion of the Iranian arms sales profits from the beginning. Mr. Casey, on the other hand, sincerely denied knowing anything of the matter until November 1986.

Then there are the other worthies. Col. North testified that Secretary of State George Shultz "knew in sufficiently eloquent terms what I had done." Not so, said the secretary's spokesman. Mr. Shultz was not "indicating either his knowledge or approval" of the colonel's Contra-aid activities. Col. North said he assumed Attorney General Edwin Meese had to know of the arms shipments to Iran as early as 1985. Mr. Meese insists he knew nothing until last November too. Assistant Secretary of State Elliott Abrams "knew" that the supply plane shot down in Nicaragua with an American on board was connected to the U.S. government, Col. North says. Absolutely not, says Mr. Abrams.

Col. North had told him he "was not violating the law."

Most of these men sound and look sincere. Certainly each one sees himself as honorable, and perhaps so are they all, all honorable men. But the public is no longer so sure. The polls say the people believe Col. North but not the president. They believe Col. North, but also believe his superiors are using him as a scapegoat.

The reason the president and the others are no longer believable is that even the best, the most sincere of performances cannot indefinitely sustain a script riddled with lies. From the first shipment of arms to Iran, American policy has been riddled with lies—lies to allies, lies to Congress, lies to the American people, as committee co-chairman Lee Hamilton put it on Tuesday. Stellar performances notwithstanding, integrity, truth and commitment to a government of checks and balances are absolutely required or the only play that really matters will inevitably go off the boards.

August 6, 1987

Donald T. Regan made a hit at the Iran-Contra hearings for a number of reasons. Most of them are pretty obvious. He was witty, calm and so clearly out of the power loop when it came to the issues under review that everyone decided to relax and enjoy the testimony with him. There were no headhunters in evidence for the simple reason that it is hard to decapitate a man carrying his own head under his arm.

Everyone had a favorite moment in those amiable two days last week, and mine came when the former White House chief of staff answered a commiserative inquiry from one of the committee members. Hadn't he really been made the classic fall guy for the Katzenjammer Kids running the president's secret government? Mr. Regan replied:

"I'm not sure I'm the fall guy in that sense of the word. As far as spears in the breast are concerned, I don't mind spears in the breast. It's knives in the back that concern me."

At the moment he said that, a wave of utter empathy, of pure, unadulterated sympathetic identification, poured over me. As he spoke, he spoke for every man and woman who ever came to Washington from that rough and tumble, relatively open world beyond the Potomac. It's a world almost unknown to the power players of the Washington swamp, a world where goals are clear and enemies open. More particularly, in that outside world, it is the exception rather than the near rule when supposed allies smile and smile and play the villain. The American ethos notwithstanding, the preferred mode of combat in the nation's capital is the shot from ambush.

To be as candid as possible about it, the usual specialists in such matters are the political appointees and their staffs. The assiduously cultivated myth of bureaucratic demons notwithstanding, a myth propagated almost always because it serves the purposes of each administration's true believers, the vast majority of all assassinations from behind are the product of staffers on their masters' business.

The knives-in-the-dark syndrome is symbolic of a larger reality here in Washington. Responsibility without power, or at least the appearance of responsibility without power, is one aspect of it. Power without responsibility, without accountability, à la Ollie North, is the other. It is not that the good Marine (or special assistant or admiral) doesn't cover his behind by making sure a superior is informed, but that both subordinate and superior operate in a sphere far removed from the normal concept of political accountability. In that sphere, where all that counts is results, the swift smear is an admired art form and visibility is the most egregious sin.

More disturbing, however, are the implications of responsibility without real power. It turns out that we were worrying about the wrong thing with Don Regan—and with George Shultz and Caspar Weinberger, for that matter. Rather than being the all-powerful and quite visible czar of the White House, Mr. Regan might just as well have been back on Wall Street. And if the secretaries of state and defense are to be believed, they were impotent in the face of the maneuvering of a handful of White House aides.

There is one other group of players in Washington that not only makes possible the dry-gulcher's world but actually encourages it—and all in the name of openness and the people's right to know. The media collectively have decided that the story is more important than anything else, including accountability, and have willingly provided the hiding place from which their sources can fire away. Having thus encouraged a tendency that does very well on its own, we in the press then step back a pace and piously decry what we have helped to promote. Such is the kingdom of the "fourth branch of government."

There are plenty of people in Washington who consider such ruminations hopelessly naive. Power and skullduggery have long been familiar bedfellows, they argue, and if the Regans of this world don't understand that, they don't deserve power. But we have rather laboriously created a system in which accountability lies at the root. If what now are to be admired and rewarded, rather than penalized, are anonymous murder and government in the shadows, we might as well abandon the system in theory as well as in fact. The Byzantines at least admitted to being what they were.

4

Defense

November 12, 1981

When it comes to the administration's new strategic weaponry program, the mountain labored and brought forth a very expensive molehill. Although no one will admit it, and many observers still don't seem to understand, President Reagan has taken a page from John F. Kennedy's book. Twenty years ago the missile gap was interred shortly after the election it helped to win; this year, the "window of vulnerability" was closed as an issue only 11 months after millions of Americans had been taught to shiver in its draft.

Actually, that isn't quite true. At his October press briefing on the subject, the president did manage to keep the window open, even if it was no longer the window of campaign days. What the window looks out upon is Soviet dominance on the European front and Moscow's vastly superior navy, the president said. Secretary of Defense Caspar Weinberger somehow managed to maintain his justly famous poker face, but over at the Pentagon, grown men were seen weeping openly and without shame.

Among the true believers at Defense, on Capitol Hill and along Pundit Row, the awful truth is almost too much to bear. The president's programs do nothing to alter America's alleged vulnerability to a Soviet first strike. Our land-based missiles will not be adequately protected, according to their doctrine, during the period of what was once called maximum peril, which is from now through the mid-1980s. The head of the Air Force's research and engineering division told Congress that "we cannot assure survivability" of the MX in the hardened Titan and Minuteman silos planned for its short-term future. The hard decisions on MX will be made in 1984, which means all the grim scenarios outlined by Ronald Reagan the campaigner will be unaffected by Ronald Reagan the president until then.

But if the MX feature of the new strategic program is a non-starter in real terms, the B1 bomber once more turns out to be a grossly overpriced turkey. On the testimony of no less an expert than Mr. Weinberger himself, it will be able to penetrate Soviet air defenses for four years at most after it is deployed. For that limited bit of defense lagniappe, the taxpayers will have to shell out up to $39 billion, even while millions and then billions of dollars are being simultaneously spent on the development of a bomber which can evade detection and hit Soviet targets.

The CIA claims that the current fleet of B52 bombers, aging though they are, will be able to accomplish their most important task through the rest of this decade and beyond. Soviet air defenses or no, they will be able to stand off from Russian air space and fire away with cruise missiles, which can make it to their destination. In other words, the B1 would be built, if it is approved, primarily so its advocates could say that it had been built, and not for any vital defense purpose.

None of this troubles the surface certainty of the administration, which continues to assert, as the president did on Tuesday, that both hardened silos and B1 bombers are necessary. Nevertheless, the suspicion grows stronger by the day that key officials on the Reagan team are well aware of the absurdity of their case and would not be grief-stricken if Congress were to say no.

If the plainly nonsensical nature of both decisions and the lukewarm enthusiasm of their sponsors are not compelling, Congress should kill the plans on the basis of cost-benefit analysis alone. Consider the figure for hardening 50 silos to temporarily house the MX, keeping in mind that Air Force experts have repeatedly said such hardened sites are vulnerable. The price is now estimated at $5 billion to $7 billion. On the basis of past Pentagon estimates that means it could eventually be twice as high—and what those dollars will buy is a big fat nothing.

If the price tag for hardening silos to no discernible effect seems monstrous, the numbers game which has been played with the 100-bomber B1 force is ludicrous. As Sen. David Pryor of Arkansas noted during a recent Senate hearing, the prime contractor of the B1 estimated early this year that it would cost $11.9 billion. In May, the Air Force said the figure might be $15 billion to $18 billion. The Defense Department then raised the ante to $19.7 billion, and Mr. Weinberger saw that figure and raised it to $21 billion—minus the inflation factor. The Congressional Budget Office this week put the cost at $39 billion. Given the record, who really doubts that estimate, the president possibly excepted? Inflation may be tapering off generally, but in the big bang department, the buck buys less and less.

Let no one suppose that defense overruns have not been a matter of Pentagon concern, however. Even while the price of some of their favorite gobblers soared skyward, Defense Department officials were bitterly resisting a Senate-passed amendment to the Defense Authorization Act which would make them accountable for their underestimates. The amendment was sponsored by Sen. Sam Nunn, a good friend of increased defense spending, precisely because he sees the handwriting on the wall. In a day of government-enforced austerity in social welfare programs, the public will not be long sympathetic to overruns larger than the cuts taken out of the safety net.

This obvious disarray offers a measure of hope for those who echo President Eisenhower's farewell concern about the "recurring temptation to feel that some spectacular and costly action could become a miraculous solution to all current difficulties."

The administration has offered a program which doesn't treat the disease it originally diagnosed and which costs far too much for the limited results it can legitimately promise. That's a prescription for political repudiation tomorrow and a more sensible approach to defense spending the day after that.

April 8, 1982

All right, folks, it's put up or shut up time on the nuclear war front. The administration has been talking out of both sides of its mouth with startling frequency of late, sometimes sounding like a dove and sometimes like a prophet of Armageddon, and the result has been widespread confusion. Perhaps that is the intended result, but the people deserve better.

What are we to make of Secretary of State Haig's preemptive strike of a speech Tuesday, in which he sought to head off the proponents both of a nuclear freeze and of a no-first-use pledge? This was not Haig the bureaucratic mumbo-jumbo man, speaking in unknown tongues under the pressure of congressional or journalistic questioning. This was the secretary of state of the United States voicing the carefully crafted words of an elaborate staff structure, words which were cleared line by line with the White House. And here are some of the things he said:

"A freeze at current levels would perpetuate an unstable and unequal military balance." That's clear enough. The Russians are ahead of us.

But no! As he rolled toward the close of his peroration, he reminded us that deterrence is "not automatic. It cannot be had on the cheap. Our ability to sustain it depends upon our ability to maintain the military balance now being threatened by the Soviet buildup." As best we understand English, to "maintain the military balance" is to perpetuate something which already exists—and that something is not our old friend of earlier paragraphs, "an unstable and unequal military balance."

Perhaps we shouldn't carp, however, since Secretary Haig finally managed to come close to saying what the president and his secretary of defense have been unable to articulate. There's no such thing as a limited nuclear war, Mr. Haig almost said.

"Flexible response is not premised upon the view that nuclear war can be controlled," he said. "Every successive allied and American government has been convinced that a nuclear war, once initiated, could escape such control." Well, "could" isn't exactly "would," but it's close enough to give everyone a whiff of the reality which lies just around the nuclear warning shot corner and just over the horizon of an exchange of tactical nuclear weapons.

The real question, however, is whether the president and his chief advisers believe an all-out nuclear war is winnable. The old reply was something along the following line, to paraphrase Defense Secretary Weinberger:

"Well, I don't think I want to answer that question, but the Russians apparently think that it is."

In the face of the burgeoning, grass-roots demand for an end to the nuclear arms race and the rhetoric which accompanies it, a new approach has been adopted. Thus, President Reagan at his press conference last week spoke the simple, unalterable truth that "I don't think there could be any winners—everybody would be a loser if there's a nuclear war." That's a declarative sentence to warm the heart of anyone concerned about man's fate.

Alas, that was not the end of it. Secretary Haig this week told the world that "deterrence depends upon our capability, even after suffering a massive nuclear blow, to prevent an aggressor from securing a military advantage and prevailing in a conflict."

What can "prevailing in a conflict" possibly mean except winning? And if our policy is actually based on the fear that someone could win a nuclear war, then the president's statement has no operational meaning. For that matter, the president's heartfelt certainty that we are behind the Russians in military might led him to contend that "they could absorb our retaliatory blow and hit us again."

To what end does all this bleak talk take us, if not a landscape of endless computer-directed nuclear exchanges and counter-exchanges, followed by the emergence of some radiation-singed survivor from his island cave to proclaim victory?

It would be unfair to suggest that America's leaders are not sincerely concerned about the prospect of nuclear war and determined to avoid it.

They deeply believe that we can get to arms reductions only by first achieving real arms parity. Unfortunately, they also apparently believe that such parity does not now exist, that the famous "window of vulnerability" goes ever before us in time, and that the "Soviet Union does have a definite margin of superiority," as the president put it in his press conference.

That way lies policy madness or policy immobilization, or both. A year-and-a-half after its election victory, the administration still has no agreed position on strategic arms control negotiations, apparently in large part because it can't reach a consensus on what strategic parity entails. That's immobilization. Lacking such an agreement, it continues to throw money at the Defense Department in hopes that it can buy what no one seems able to define. That's madness, a fact well understood by the markets and our allies.

And in the meantime what one rhetorical hand gives, the other takes away, and we are left with the indelible impression that the people who run this country believe that the Soviet Union really is 10-feet tall, intends to launch a nuclear war just as soon as it has an appropriate edge in land-based missiles and might actually survive the ensuing holocaust as the "winner." It's almost enough to make even the most dedicated civil defense skeptic take up a shovel and start digging.

November 7, 1982

In a political year, some things are to be expected. For instance, with automobile sales at a 21-year low and unemployment at a post-World War II high and climbing, the party in power will engage in as much sleight of hand as possible. Trying to switch the public's attention to another subject when the one at hand is politically painful is an old, if not precisely honorable, tradition in our country. Everybody does it.

But there are disturbing indications that the president and some of his supporters have decided to pull out all the stops on this approach and transform it from something that is relatively silly to something less amusing. Sen. Jeremiah Denton (R., Ala.) played one variation on this mutt's game late last week. Mr. Reagan played a louder, more strident rendition while campaigning in the economic wasteland of the Midwest this week.

The senator, who was promptly rebuked by several of his colleagues, noted the presence of what he termed "groups that are openly critical of, even hostile to . . . our country" among those supporting an organization called Peace Links. His was a pathetic echo of one of Sen. Denton's spiritual godfathers, Joe McCarthy, and can be dismissed as just one more bit of extremist malarkey from a mediocre pol.

Then along came the only president we have, Mr. Nice Guy himself, who said of protesters favoring a nuclear freeze:

"They were demonstrating in behalf of a movement that has swept across our country that I think is inspired by not the sincere and honest people who want peace but by some who want the weakening of America, and so are manipulating many honest and sincere people."

So, as best that sentence can be interpreted, the motivating force behind the peace movement is a faceless clutch of folks who want the "weakening of America." And who could they be? Well, the president didn't say and knew he didn't have to say to get the message across, but we'll spell it out for the dimwitted and those too young to remember the 1950s. The communists are responsible for the freeze movement. In other words, as Sen. Denton put it more forthrightly, it's made in Moscow.

This won't do, and someone should persuade the president to drop it before it poisons the political process in a way that makes today's economic difficulties seem manageable. It won't do despite the kernel of truth that can be found at the bottom of this particular barrel: That is, the truth that some individuals and groups that have been extremely responsive to every twist and turn in the official Soviet line can be found lined up behind the nuclear freeze. Hard as it may be for some people, including the president, to believe, that neither invalidates the freeze thesis nor proves that it is a Russian product.

Perhaps a little reasoning by analogy would help. The president, both as candidate and president, has expressed certain positions on civil rights issues which are identical to the position of the Ku Klux Klan. He, like the Klan, is opposed to court-ordered busing and affirmative action programs that involve quotas and, until convinced otherwise, was opposed to the extension of a toughened Voting Rights Act. The Klan's leadership has backed him on every point, as well as publicly endorsing him for president in 1980.

Does that mean the president's civil rights stance is Klan inspired? Does it mean he is a Klan dupe? Are those in the political reaches of the Justice Department and elsewhere who believe there should be an alternative to activist government intervention on behalf of human rights not "sincere and honest people" who also want a just society, but merely "some who want the weakening" of the drive for full equality under the law? Is the president himself a racist, given his bedfellows on these matters?

Such questions enrage the president and infuriate his non-racist supporters, while elevating the Klan's importance far above its real significance. To be fair about it, the president is entitled to fury. The issues raised by his racial policies should be debated on their merits and not on the basis of guilt by association.

To get down to cases, the nuclear freeze movement is led and overwhelmingly populated by men and women whose one and only political allegiance is to their country, and who are motivated far more by religious conviction or moral concern for man's fate than by any ideology, foreign or domestic. That is why, as the president correctly noted, it has "swept across our country."

Nor is it a given truth that the Russians are so positioned in strategic weaponry that a freeze "would bring closer a chance of nuclear war," as the president keeps insisting. In the real world, in which one of our more than 40 invulnerable nuclear submarines has enough deliverable power to cause 48 million Russian deaths and in which we have 30,000 nuclear warheads of one kind or another, it is ludicrous to suppose there is anyone in the Kremlin who actually thinks there is such a thing as a winnable nuclear war. Conversely, what the freeze advocates say is that it is the constantly spiraling arms race, sustained in pursuit of the ever-receding illusion of national security through mounting stockpiles of doomsday bombs, that is responsible for bringing closer the "chance of nuclear war."

That's in the realm of fair debate and persons of unimpeachable integrity and impressive expertise can be found on both sides of it. It is also a legitimate campaign issue on which the people deserve reasoned discussion and information. To resurrect the red herring from its smelly grave, however, is to perform a profound disservice to the republic. The Lord (and Mr. Reagan) knows that times are bad enough as they are. They will get infinitely worse if the White House embarks on a deliberate campaign of Red scare.

December 27, 1984

The president called five U.S. servicemen stationed abroad on Christmas Day, a nice touch showing those five at least that the nation's leader appreciates their efforts. In our family, we all took turns talking to my son, who is in Kenya with the Peace Corps.

It undoubtedly added to his Christmas. It made ours.

And both sets of conversations reminded me of two other highly personal Christmas Day communications from days past. One was with my wife 26 years ago, when a particularly miserable young lieutenant had the duty at Camp Lejeune and couldn't spend the holiday with his wife and infant daughter. The other was 44 years ago, when Dad was in training with his newly activated National Guard unit at Camp Blanding, Fla., and he sent home one of those scratchy records you could cut in a booth telling his wife and two sons how much he missed them.

I mention these tales of 1958 and 1940 not because they are of any intrinsic interest to people outside my immediate family, but because of something they say about the vast changes that have taken place in this country since the years immediately preceding World War II.

Dad was one of a handful of citizen soldiers under arms before Pearl Harbor, and he was there because he had decided that the war was coming and each American had a responsibility to do something about it. President Roosevelt agreed enough to activate that particular Guard division, made up of Deep Southern boys and men, over a year before the U.S. actually entered the fighting. And I was in the Marine Corps in 1958 because when I went to Princeton in the early 1950s, it was as normal for many undergraduates to join the ROTC as it is for many undergraduates today to go directly into graduate school, whether they had (or have) any real calling in that direction or not.

In 1940, there was still a great national division over the proper role the U.S. should play in the world, Axis powers or no Axis powers. By 1958, there was virtually no debate in America about the right and necessity of our country doing everything possible to "defend the free world," as we liked to put it, and this included calling on men from all walks of life—including Princeton graduates—to help do just that.

That is not the dominant theme when it comes to national defense today, nor has it been for well over a decade. This nation has a standing military force of over two million men and women, but the vast majority of all Americans who are 40 or younger have no sense that the armed forces have anything to do with them. Many, if not most, enthusiastically cheer the much heralded "new awakening" of patriotism going on around them, but the cheering dies away when someone suggests that national service should be the shared burden of all. "Billions for defense" is the new American motto, with an implicit footnote: But not my kids.

This dominant sub-theme first became apparent to me during the mid-1960s, when the fervor of some folks' hawkish views on Vietnam was matched only by their ingenuity in avoiding service, or helping their kids avoid service, there. The number of ardent patriots who rushed to join the National Guard and Reserve—not because they thought it would get them to the front, but because they were sure it would keep them from it—was legion. The draft-dodging devices used by the anti-war activists were obvious and openly proclaimed. Those adopted by the sunshine patriots, some of whom serve as all-out defense advocates in Congress today, were more devious but no less effective. By the end of the war, the kids doing the fighting and dying were overwhelmingly drawn from the ranks of America's have-nots.

To ensure that this would be the way of national service thenceforth, the then-Republican president and the then-liberal Democratic congressional majority joined hands to kill the draft and create a "volunteer" military establishment. From that moment to this, a process has been under way that is dangerous to the country as a whole and damaging both to the larger civilian society and to the smaller military one. We are, consciously or unconsciously, creating two utterly separate worlds, inhabiting the same space but sharing fewer and fewer common bonds.

One is made up of those who have chosen to make the military their life. The other is made up of those who zealously avoid touching anything to do with the military. And the gulf of perception and viewpoint that separates the two grows larger with each year. For one, national service is the highest calling. For the other, national service is a bad joke, an imposition, or a relic of a barely remembered past. And even those who go in and come out after one tour of duty know they live in a different environment from their peers who never wore a uniform.

And so, unfortunately, when the president made his Christmas calls on behalf of the nation, the people he talked to were not representative of all Americans, nor could they feel they were engaged in some shared purpose with all Americans. Most Americans no longer seem to believe that defense should be a common enterprise, or if they believe it, that the sharing should go beyond their tax dollars. The five men with whom the president talked were serving in posts all over the world, but none were as distant from most Americans as is the fact that they are in the armed forces in the first place.

February 7, 1985

The president has invoked the Lord on behalf of his defense-spending plans, which will add $2 trillion over the next five years to an already swollen program. Some observers have asked whether that doesn't cast doubt on his more mundane justifications for the big-bucks, big-bang, small-heart budget he has submitted to Congress. Whatever the explanation, the resort to Scripture makes more sense than the defense budget itself. Having decided that you can't buy domestic security by throwing dollars at every problem, the U.S. is proving that throwing dollars at every weapons system has little relationship to true national security.

But, as noted in Ecclesiastes, "There is no new thing under the sun." Since the Cold War's dawn, the reality of the Soviet challenge has been stretched to incorporate the supposedly imminent threat of Soviet superiority. From bomber gap to missile gap, from the image of Red hordes poised for a strike across Europe, we have been fed the Chicken Little scenario, and repeatedly Congress and the people have funded what the Pentagon demanded.

Just as repeatedly, later examination showed that the "gaps" resulted from someone's nightmares rather than good intelligence. And while the Soviet Union's or its proxies' forces are in Angola, Afghanistan and Ethiopia, they are no longer in Egypt, Somalia and about a half-dozen other nations once thought lost to Moscow's designs. Today, we, not Russia, have a military relationship with China.

But perhaps that should be regarded as old business, of no relevance to the realities of the 1980s. As we were instructed repeatedly during the mid- and late-1970s, a new peril threatened. It was the "window of vulnerability," the result of alleged failures to match the Russians' strategic buildup between 1965 and 1976. Almost inevitably, Moscow would exploit that window by pouring its heavy missiles through and wiping out our land-based missiles in one all-or-nothing strike. The antidote? The president's military spending plans.

Four years later, we are either enjoying a new balance of forces in our favor (Secretary of State George Shultz), rapidly catching up (the president), or in continued peril (Secretary of Defense Caspar Weinberger). Whatever we are, however, we are in that state without any of the new strategic toys the believers in the present danger said were absolutely essential for our security. The MX is still not deployed, Midgetman is a theory, the new bombers are prototypes rather than assembly-line products and virtually every other system given the go-ahead by the Reagan administration is still somewhere in the long pipeline.

But no one talks about the "window of vulnerability" anymore because it never existed. We had in 1980 what we have now, more than adequate retaliatory resources in our "antique" B-52 bombers, long-distance nuclear submarines and highly accurate land-based missiles. Beyond that, the only new systems that have come on line in any numbers were the results of Carter-administration decisions. A majority of all ships added since 1980, the cruise missiles being deployed by the thousands, and the policy basis for the deployment of new Pershings and cruise missiles in Europe: All had their origins in the 1977–80 period.

Since then, the defense budget has been pumped up almost geometrically, with much of the new money set for the new systems so loved by the individual services. There is already a backlog of well over $200 billion in unspent funds, and the 1986–88 projections seek authorization of more than a trillion more. That spending should be balanced against a recent story in the Wall Street Journal, which estimated that Soviet military expenditures this year might reach $45 billion (adjusting for hidden costs). Double that again, to $90 billion or $100 billion, and you still come up with radically different rates of defense spending imposed against a pre-existing background of strategic equivalency.

There is much talk about a stiffening of Congress's spine. It is being suggested that in a day of deep cutbacks in so many domestic programs and a $2 trillion national debt, there is no way that the Hill will go along with a 10% boost for the military. Perhaps that is so, although the record of the past four years casts doubt on the proposition. Congress approved more than 95% of Mr. Reagan's military spending requests in his first term, and that approval built in almost 40% of the estimated defense budget for the next fiscal year.

The circle can be broken, but it will take a conceptual rather than pencil-sharpening approach. A hint of the way it could and should go was offered by Rep. Les Aspin, chairman of the House Armed Services Committee. As he put it: "In the boldest terms, what we must tell the Defense Department is, 'Before we give you billions more, we want to know what you've done with the trillion you've got.' What I would like the committee to do is step back and take a broad look at the whole program—what we have accomplished and what we have yet to do."

In other words, a debate about the structure of defense rather than a nibbling of the edges. Without such a comprehensive method, the president's approach will necessarily prevail. With or without the Lord's intervention, the inertia of events in post-war America is almost always in favor of spending for defense first and thinking about what is really needed second.

October 16, 1986

It is generally accepted that no one can play the game of "spin the ball" better than Ronald Reagan and his public-relations team. Thus there was a swap that wasn't a swap, a summit that wasn't a summit and a failure that wasn't a failure. It is hard to conceive of the limits to which rhetoric might have soared if Iceland had actually produced results.

Mr. Gorbachev's Kremlin is playing catch-up in Madison Avenue techniques, so the propaganda artifice on both sides is wider and deeper than ever before. On the one hand there is the theme of paradise lost. On the other is the blame-game, with each calling the other responsible for the loss of that nuclear-free Eden. The "deal that almost was" is rapidly entering the world of myth populated by Santa Claus and the Easter bunny.

In the short run, it probably will come out a wash. The Soviets will get at least some mileage out of their accusation that Mr. Reagan's intransigence on the Strategic Defense Initiative was alone responsible for blocking agreement. That will find resonance in some quarters, since in fact the summit did finally break down because the president would not use his cherished SDI as a bargaining chip.

And the president obviously has carried the day in Europe and at home for the moment. The message is that Iceland was not the last, best hope, but was actually the first day of the rest of arms control's life. The deafening criticism you don't hear from the Democrats demonstrates just how effective the administration blitz has been. History may say that the summit was an unequivocal failure, but that is tomorrow's judgment. Today, "how near" is the catch phrase, not "how far."

Yet everyone ought to be breathing a sigh of relief. The dream of a no-nuke world is a worthy one, but for the foreseeable future it is unobtainable in reality and unwise in theory. Hard as it is for Ronald Reagan, the visionary hawk, and the whole dovecote of nuclear disarmers to accept, the nuclear balance of terror remains the best bulwark against World War III anyone has been able to devise. That is not an argument for a never-ending arms race. It is, however, an unambiguous case for arms-control agreements that leave each side certain that all-out war would incinerate both homelands.

In the best of all possible worlds, that would mean a situation in which each country had about 100 utterly invulnerable missiles targeted on the other. There could be no escape and no victory. There would therefore be no temptation to strike.

But isn't that just what mutual assured destruction (MAD) has been all about, and doesn't just about everyone profess to hate it as immoral, unthinkable and unworkable? Yes and yes. But they are wrong. The big peace has been maintained exactly because of a shared understanding of the consequences of the big war. This has been demoralizing and frightening, but so far the key word has been living.

But why isn't that a justification of the arms race? And why isn't it an argument against any kind of arms-control agreement at all? On the first, because the central point of MAD is the word assured. The arms race continually raises the possibility that one of the players might make such a significant technological breakout that he would be tempted to go for a first strike. While that is as unlikely in the real world as a leak-proof space shield, it keeps planners awake nights on both sides and thinking of new ways to get there first.

On the second, the reason for trying to reduce the scope of weapons on both sides, while protecting or guaranteeing their invulnerability, is that it helps validate the deterrence guarantee. It takes fingers off hair triggers—long the implicit objective of arms negotiations. It still should be.

Instead, we have the extraordinary leaps into totally unplanned fancy envisioned in the "potential" breakthroughs of Iceland. Ignore the consequences of a nuclear-free great-power rivalry at the end of 10 years; either a huge conventional-force buildup in the West or surrender on Soviet terms. Focus instead on the ludicrous notion of a world in which at least a dozen nations would have the capacity to build and deliver nuclear weapons while only the two most powerful would be formally without them. Or, as an alternative, try to envision how France or China could be persuaded to abandon its independent deterrents. France has been known to blow up sailing vessels for less cause.

The administration has spent the past few days saying that things aren't as bad as they initially seemed, that much is still salvageable. That's called putting a spin on the ball, but the spin is about half right. Because of SDI, the wrong reason, we avoided the wrong outcome. Unfortunately, because of SDI, deep cuts in heavy missiles don't seem likely until a new president makes a new appraisal of the whole idea. But flesh was put on the bones of an agreement in Iceland on intermediate-range missiles, and if both leaders are serious, they should be able to breathe new life into its body. On that one, the burden is almost entirely on the Soviets, who once seemed to promise a willingness to make an agreement in that area without requiring an agreement elsewhere.

Beyond that possible positive outcome, the rapture-at-Reykjavik myth is dangerous. It encourages the president in his worst tendency, which is to argue for all or nothing on strategic arms reductions. The big fix isn't in the cards and never has been, but the small fixes that promote stability are always available to those with the wit to promote them.

5

Reaganism Abroad

April 30, 1981

The question must be asked: What is the Reagan administration's definition of America's role in the world?

It must be asked and it should be answered, assuming the president's foreign policy team is ever officially selected and confirmed, because it is the critical factor in the current debate over defense spending. (Perhaps debate isn't the right word, given the capitulation of the opposition to the notion that more defense spending is better, and much, much more is great.)

To this outsider, at least, the president and his men seem to have resurrected the thesis that we can and should play world policeman. They define our world role in essentially negative terms. That is, the United States' chief interest is to block and defeat Soviet objectives.

That belief is matched by an overwhelming tendency to see the Soviet hand behind every insurrection and every demand for political change. The president spoke directly to that point when, as a candidate, he said:

"Let's not delude ourselves. The Soviet Union underlies all the unrest that is going on."

If the man who is now president believes that, the sky is the limit on American interventionism and military spending. Unrest, caused by economic deprivation, physical abuse, political repression and official as well as unofficial terrorism, is going to be a fact of life in scores of countries for decades to come. If the central thrust of our foreign policy is to counter the Soviet Union, and if the Soviet Union is the primary agent of internal unrest everywhere, then we will be intervening from the Halls of Montezuma to the Shores of Tripoli.

The new projected $336 billion defense budget five years hence won't begin to cover the cost of such an approach. Our standing military will have to be doubled at a minimum. The draft will have to be reinstituted.

Perhaps this projection is overheated and overdrawn. But there is more recent evidence than a candidate's oratory to suggest that it isn't.

For instance, as best as can be interpreted from the statements of Secretary of State Haig, the president, National Security Adviser Richard Allen and others, some speaking behind the curtain of confidentiality, the United States believes that our vital national interests are currently involved in:

Southern Africa, to the point that aiding anti-government forces in Angola and pro-government forces in South Africa is once more being considered.

The Persian Gulf, to the extent that we are willing to enrage an old friend, Israel, by loading up a newer friend, Saudi Arabia, with weaponry which is irrelevant to its real security needs. At the same time Washington talks of a long-term, multi-billion military aid arrangement with Pakistan, that shaky pillar of stability in Southwest Asia.

The Middle East, where the real threat to peace is said to come not from fundamental differences between the Arab states and Israel, but from Soviet machinations.

Central America, where the bloody, bitter civil war in El Salvador is presented as a vital test of our ability to turn a Moscow-powered revolutionary tide in the region.

South America, where the perceived need for good anti-Communist friends means re-establishing warm and supportive relations with various repressive dictatorships of the right, and presumably backing them whenever they are threatened by internal difficulties.

Europe, both West and East, to the extent that we must exhort our allies to consider more closely their own peril while warning Moscow continually against imperiling either its erstwhile satraps or its longtime NATO adversaries.

It is hard to avoid the suspicion that Washington hasn't identified all of Asia as vital to our security as well only because it hasn't gotten around to it yet.

The United States does have important interests in a number

of places. The Soviet Union clearly tries to exploit openings and create turmoil wherever it can. But what is troubling is a world view which not only sees the red hand everywhere, but which has an unlimited notion of our responsibility to counter it.

The testimony of Undersecretary of State Walter Stoessel in support of additional assistance to the El Salvador junta was instructive:

"Experience has shown, however, that for our support to be credible, it must respond not only to the present situation but to the potential of the other side to create further violence."

Stoessel was speaking specifically of El Salvador, but he caught the administration's apparently open-ended commitment to meet the other side's "potential" anywhere and everywhere.

Caspar Weinberger, the Secretary of Defense, spoke on March 4, of the need for a vastly increased defense budget. He said in part:

"Today, the budget is not sufficient for our strategic needs. It is clearly inadequate to support our widespread commitments in peacetime. Further, it constrains our ability to meet challenges to our interests in time of crisis."

The questions arise. What are our priority "strategic needs"? What "widespread commitments" are we being asked to honor and what new ones are contemplated? What are mortal "challenges" to our interests and which are peripheral?

Without answers, the American people are being asked to hand over a blank check to finance undefined and possibly unknown objectives. We've been down that road before, and it led to disaster.

October 15, 1981

The royal We has reappeared in Washington after an absence of less than a decade. The elected leader of the United States, at last glance a mere republican (as well as Republican) president, has begun to talk in concert with his minions in terms more reminiscent of king and court than of an administration existing within the context of constitutional checks and balances.

Extraordinary rhetorical commitments are being made in our name from and on behalf of the White House. The president informed us during his press conference two weeks ago, that "we would not permit (Saudi Arabia) to be an Iran," an assertion the assembled White House reporters almost allowed to pass without follow-up, clarification or explanation. His vicar, Secretary of State Alexander Haig, has told Egypt that the United States considers Cairo's fate to be our fate and that we will not let internal change or external aggression change its allegiance. Gen. Haig did (according to Sudan's President Numeiri) or did not (according, the next day, to Mr. Haig himself) tell Sudan that the United States would fight by its side if Libya were to attack. Administration spokesmen, on and off-the-record, have lately taken to practicing their manual dexterity by drawing lines in the dust and daring freedom's enemies to cross them.

None of this is occurring in a vacuum. Recent events provide the chaotic, obviously dangerous background for the administration's exercises in public diplomacy. The assassination of President Sadat has placed all Middle Eastern equations in jeopardy. Those who fish best in troubled waters have their lines out. It is important that the United States be perceived as a steady, resolute friend in need by those who openly or privately depend on us.

Also in the background, although of less overriding importance, is the reality that the Awacs sale to Saudi Arabia barely has its nose above water on Capitol Hill. The president's men are frantically searching for a formula to satisfy enough of those who oppose the sale and snatch victory from all-but-certain defeat. A pledge that Saudi Arabia's monarchy will not, unlike Iran's, collapse under the weight of too many advanced weapons and too little advanced communication with its people must have been considered necessary to the process.

But there are several problems with all this, not the least being that no president, no secretary of state and no White House spokesman can commit America to war or, Canute-like, stand against the tide and guarantee that another nation's government will not fall or change radically. Somewhere along the line in the past 36 years, I thought that lesson had been finally learned, even if the preceding century and a half of constitutional government and American involvement in world affairs could be forgotten.

For those who need a refresher, however, by Constitution and by statute there are rigorous restrictions on a president's unilateral right to commit American troops to combat or American assistance to anyone. By the facts of sovereignty and the even more inexorable realities of history, there is often very little that one nation can do to "save" another nation's regime or dictate its internal course, short of armed occupation and savage repression. And, by virtue of our peculiar form of government in which Congress is given a major voice in the conduct of affairs both within and without the nation's borders, a presidential pledge is not the final statement on American foreign policy, for better or for worse. Ask Woodrow Wilson.

Which makes the reappearance of the language of the Imperial Presidency on the Potomac all the more interesting. In effect, the people and their Congress are being told that Papa knows best and should be trusted to do what is best for his children. A policy rebuff for the president is to be understood as a slap in the entire nation's face. As former President Jimmy Carter so obligingly put it on behalf of his former political foe, the Awacs' sale "has become the litmus test of American reliability." In other words, what the president promises, no matter how wrong, the president must be allowed to deliver, even if he didn't consult Congress in advance and even if a majority in Congress sincerely believes that making good on the promise would be the prelude to disaster.

That's a bad theory and bad government. It isn't Congress's responsibility to give a blank check after the fact to any president. It would be irresponsibility of the highest order for Congress to swallow its doubts and endorse any policy whose consequences it fears. That way lies the quagmire.

Beyond its apparent insistence that Congress should simply stand aside once the president makes a decision, the administration is wrong on another count. Frantic deployments of B-52s to Egypt will not still fundamentalist unrest. Marine amphibious landings in Oman and Somalia will not bring stability to the Persian Gulf or pacify the Horn of Africa. The Awacs will no more guarantee Saudi Arabia's territorial integrity and survival than the Awacs could have guaranteed the Shah's.

The process of encumbering the sovereign's divine right was long and painful. The Constitution was written by men who understood why no one should be given the right to reign and rule alone. Now, when the chief executive seems tempted to speak like a wartime commander in chief, if not ex cathedra, Congress must remind itself, the people and the president why the Constitution was written in the form we have inherited. Blackstone wrote in 18th century England, "That the king can do no wrong is a necessary and fundamental principle of the English constitution." We fought and won a revolution to prove that it was not the fundamental principle of this land.

May 5, 1983

The voice of the neo-Democrat is abroad in the land, urging a me-too foreign policy on the opposition party. The arguments are persuasively presented, but the logic evaporates on examination. What is advocated is capitulation to the president's fundamental premises—which is to say, to ideological slogans which pass for policy.

A few weeks ago, two officeholders in former Democratic administrations wrote a prescription for Democrats in the New York Times Sunday Magazine which read like a parody of Polonius' advice in "Hamlet." You know, as in "neither a borrower nor a lender be" and "give every man thine ear, but few thy voice." Except what they were saying went something more like, "Stand up for human rights, but not too ardently."

Then, in one of his standard virtuoso performances, Ben Wattenberg of the Committee for a Democratic Majority and other neo-Democratic causes, reappeared in print this week to warn party members against straying too far from the president's Central American policy. To do other than offer constructive embellishments on Mr. Reagan's themes is to invite inevitable political reprisal in a replay of "who lost China," Mr. Wattenberg argued.

If asked, the neo-conservatives, the accommodaters and the "realists" wouldn't agree that they are in the same camp, and at least superficially they are not.

But they share an unstated premise nonetheless. They believe that it would be wrong as well as fruitless for the Democrats to try to fashion a comprehensive foreign policy which challenges the president in fundamental, decisive ways on the basic issues of our times.

Thus the Democrats shouldn't seize the nuclear issue and fashion a tough, constructive alternative (leaving the initiative to the Catholic bishops and others) to the mindlessness of bargaining-chip proliferation. Or, they would echo with approval Henry Kissinger's remark of last week that it is time Democrats "stopped arguing only about how much democracy there is in El Salvador and began to understand America's strategic interests are at stake." In the Middle East, Southern Africa, Asia and even Europe, they recommend what amounts to tinkering with administration policies rather than the across-the-board repudiation they deserve.

There are two reasons that this approach is dead wrong. One is political. The other is more substantive.

Politically, the history of the Republican resurgence and Democratic decline of recent years has demonstrated that sharply focused ideas will dominate the public debate every time. The Republican right was in the wilderness for a long time, but when it emerged, it did so with an arsenal of policy positions which took on the conventional (which meant Democratic) wisdom with relish and skill. The Democrats, having long ago given themselves over to coalitional pragmatism which encouraged almost everything but original thought, were routed on the playing fields they once dominated. But the advice now emerging from the neo-Democrats would expand rather than contract the vacuum at the party's center. And why should the people, having the original in office, settle for some tepid imitation?

Substantively, the best argument for articulating clear alternatives to the administration's foreign policy is that it is a total, flaming disaster. The furrowed brows of establishment thinking keep suggesting that the verdict is not yet in, that events could yet turn around, but they cannot disguise their deep disquiet, or the deeply disquieting realities. There is no place that American foreign policy is working. The economic summit at Williamsburg at the end of the month will escape being a fiasco only if it is nothing at all. Thanks to its playpen shrillness, its near hysterical trumpetings about the Red peril, the administration has managed the near-impossible, which is to make the Soviet's elephantine propaganda apparatus seem to be the model of efficient sophistication.

The Middle East is a disaster area, thanks in large part to a total misreading by this government of the real objectives of most of the countries in the area. China now plays the triangular game with a vengeance. South Africa has done the obvious, picked up our conciliatory marbles, said thanks very much and continued to stall on Namibia while working overtime to destabilize its neighbors. In South America, the dictators for whom this administration displayed such tender solicitude are in disarray, disgrace or advance stages of failure from Chile to Argentina to Uruguay, but their people will long remember where we stood during the dark days of oppression.

And yet, in the face of these multiple failures, Democrats are warned not to put too much distance between themselves and the president. The advice is nonsense. When something has collapsed, you replace it. What has again collapsed is the foreign policy approach best exemplified by Henry Kissinger's remark. The proper alternative would stand his admonition on its head: Our interests in the region (and I would say, in the world) are imperiled because we have been too little interested in real democracy and too much interested in playing "strategic interests." The result has been a string of bad bets on the wrong horses, from Nationalist China to the colonels of Central America. In that sense, we "lost" China and could "lose" El Salvador. If the stands aren't applauding and the nag won't run, it's absurd to keep sending bad money after good. That's the message the Democrats should be sending to the people.

September 15, 1983

A nation commits an atrocity. Hundreds of innocents die. What is laughingly called the rule of law is ripped into small pieces and the perpetrator glares defiantly at its critics. What can be done? What should be done? The questions arose this month, after the Russians committed a monumentally barbaric act, but they confront us more regularly than we sometimes imagine. The answers, and the record of response, are not very heartening.

With the downing of KAL Flight 007, the Soviet Union did

again what it does most consistently. It behaved in a straightforwardedly brutal way to defend what it regards as its basic interests, then stared down the world. The West, including the U.S., in turn has done what it does most consistently, which is to dither about in the unwavering face of Soviet brutality and do little.

The president's reaction, a mixture of tough talk and mild measures, outraged his oldest, most loyal supporters and relieved his oldest, most severe critics. Obviously, he was wrestling with the reality that confronts every president in the nuclear age. The constraints on what one great power can do to punish the other are many, not the least being the suicidal nature of total war today. The willingness of our friends and allies to retaliate even symbolically is extremely limited.

Even so, it doesn't automatically follow that those who applauded the president were right and those who criticized him were wrong. To see murder go unpunished rubs hard against the grain, just as the Soviets' now unchallenged occupation of Afghanistan (and the long-ago collapse of sanctions) is an affront to everything many of us were taught to believe about the proper response to aggression.

It didn't require the downing of the Korean airliner to remind us that gangsterism of one kind or another seems to be endemic in today's world. The order of things is dominated by aggression and violence, along with the unwillingness of the so-called world community to respond to what the gangsters are doing, whatever their ideological pretensions or size.

In the Persian Gulf, one of the world's bloodiest wars drags on between Iran and Iraq, and there is no disposition at the U.N. or elsewhere to try to force a resolution. In Lebanon, those who call themselves Christians and those who call themselves Moslems are busily slaughtering each other with a fine disregard for their faiths' most important tenets, and with open assistance from their neighbors. The Vietnamese occupation and suppression of Cambodia elicits yawns from virtually everyone. The same was true of Indonesia's seizure of East Timor and subsequent bloody repression. Central America is drowning in its peoples' blood, with the U.S. among those supplying the tools of the killers' trade. To say the words Namibia, Chad, Chile and the Philippines is to conjure up images of bloodshed, despotism, tribal warfare and unrelenting hatred.

That is where some experts leave it. Having concurred in the itemization, they hurriedly add that we cannot "impose our values" abroad. Others observe that there are times and places where, despite all our power, we are powerless to alter events or force nations to do our will, whether over the Sea of Japan or in the Middle East. They note that the world has grown more dangerous, and that even as our armed might has dramatically increased, our ability to influence others appears to have diminished.

Finally, there are the selective realists. If they are of the left, they argue for "calm maturity" in our dealings with the Soviet Union, no matter what it may do, while simultaneously advocating retaliation, economic and political, against repressive right-wing regimes. If they are of the right, they are ready to call down anathema against Communist nations when they transgress international norms, but believe we must be "realistic" when our self-professed friends butcher their own subjects in the name of anti-communism.

And there is the key to the proper approach for this country, whether in the wake of the downing of KAL 007 or the deliberate assassination of Benigno Aquino by the Marcos regime. We can admit that there is a limit to our effective power, but nonetheless insist on making crystal clear our repugnance and repudiation of what has occurred. It is imperative that Washington not reward murderers with business as usual, even if that means the U.S. must go it alone in what it does. Yes, Ronald Reagan should have done more to drive home this nation's reaction to the destruction of the Korean 747, just as he should do far more to let our clients in El Salvador, the Philippines and elsewhere know that we do not endorse official murder. Such an approach may or may not bring immediate results, but it does distance the world's most powerful country from those who believe in the law of the jungle. If we are not willing to speak and act forcefully, across the board, when the gangsters strike, who will?

September 27, 1984

It's great fun to boom out the bombast at political conventions dominated by flag-waving believers in the big-stick, big-megaphone approach to foreign policy. Surges of adrenalin are released by chanting loud mantras to the restoration of American strength and the toughening of American will. Cheering enthusiasm greets the pledge that "Americans will never again be held hostage," and that a blow against us anywhere in the world will bring certain reprisal. How psychically rewarding are all those muscular words—and how empty the deeds.

Which is not to say there is anything remotely funny about

the ability of terrorists to strike with lethal impunity at the heart of the U.S. presence in Beirut, not once but three times. There is nothing even slightly amusing about the fact that three, perhaps four, Americans are held hostage in Lebanon by well-known thugs.

But it is grotesquely funny to watch the administration's most famous mouth-that-roars, U.N. Ambassador Jeane Kirkpatrick, offer banal, lame cliches when confronted with her government's impotence, as she was on ABC's David Brinkley show last Sunday. Criticism of that impotence, she was finally reduced to insinuating, is really just a product of the "blame America" crowd. That kind of intellectual garbage may play well before GOP delegates in Dallas, but it bombs elsewhere. As ABC newsman Sam Donaldson remarked to the ambassador, while she once proudly announced that the Reagan administration had taken the "kick-me sign" off the door, America had received mortal blows repeatedly and no one had kicked back.

Saying that the president has no clothes is an infinitely rewarding exercise in truth telling, but it doesn't bear too much repetition. While his administration doesn't deserve a break that it wouldn't give its foes and that Mr. Reagan didn't give his predecessor, the president is hoist on a petard that was launched long before he came to power. There are limited options available to tough talkers no less than mild ones when it comes to terrorism in particular and the flow of events in most other countries in general.

The president seems momentarily more willing to face that reality today than his old stump speeches or the claptrap of the GOP platform might lead you to believe. Suddenly we are asked to remember that terrorism is hard to counter, harder still to uncover in advance. We are asked to be tolerant of repeated security lapses. We are told by unidentified administration spokesmen that rescue efforts could endanger the lives of the hostages, who might as well be faceless for all that official Washington wants to talk about them.

We are, in short, back in the world of President Carter and the Iranian hostage crisis, and for good reason. There aren't many useful ways to apply the kind of power our government has built at astronomical expense. Conceding that, which means conceding that we have constructed a multibillion-dollar fighting machine with limited utility in real-world situations, is hard to do, but it's the beginning of wisdom. Intelligent policy can flow only from a willingness to concede that retreaded battleships, nuclear missiles and supertanks are irrelevant to almost every conceivable crisis the U.S. is likely to face.

For that matter, terrorism itself is not easily beaten by force alone, although it is imperative that firmness and force be employed. If an eye for an eye were all that it took, Israel long since would have eliminated the problem. Instead, while instant retaliation is the official policy and its success is widely proclaimed, Israel has not and cannot end terrorism that way, although it can make it costly. The reason is that there are more recruits for the cause spread across the Middle East than there are Israeli bullets to kill them. Until the excuse for such murderous fanaticism is eradicated, terrorism will remain.

It's not actually true that firepower alone can't end or severely curtail terrorism. If a nation is able and willing, it can invade a country, impose military rule and ruthlessly control the countryside until most resistance is eliminated. That is the way that the Soviet Union seeks to control the "terrorists" of Afghanistan.

Thus it is possible to construct a theoretical case that we could solve our problems in Lebanon or El Salvador or Nicaragua or in any other outpost of what the administration sees as our proper sphere of influence, if we put enough troops on the ground. It would change the definition of what we were doing, and indeed of what this country is all about, but it is at least theoretically possible.

But if that is not what the administration intends, it should face up to the facts, drop the bluster and start searching for nonmilitary answers to what are fundamentally nonmilitary problems. It should stop pretending that a hard blow here or a hard word there will suffice and stop acting on the failed theory that the U.S., or any other power, can successfully impose its will on a distant people for any length of time without intolerable cost. It should talk sense to the American people and admit the unpalatable, which is that there are and should be limits to American power. But that is a phrase the president believes he was elected to extirpate from Washington's vocabulary, and so we apparently are doomed to a dreary cycle of harsh rhetoric and overreaching commitment followed by failed policy and ignominious retreat.

December 13, 1984

Slowly, on the little cats' feet of all deliberate speed, the president of the United States seems to be moving toward accommodation with the notion that a democratic society has an obligation to speak and act in the world as though it believed in its own principles.

The operative words, of course, are "slowly" and "seems," but the movement is nonetheless there to be seen. In taking Monday's anniversary, of the Universal Declaration of Human Rights as the moment for a modest, modulated public denunciation of South Africa's unyielding policy of apartheid, Mr. Reagan broke with his own past and his administration's most cherished human-rights principle, which is that Washington should speak out vigorously against human-rights abuses only when they are committed by Moscow or its minions.

Cynics may protest that we should not make an endless summer out of one or two swallows, and there is ample justification for such restrained reaction. In past years, the mangy dogs embraced by the White House in the name of "free world" solidarity have had to engage in naked political murder (the Philippines) or show an unseemly reluctance to punish the killers of American civilians (El Salvador) before the administration's spokesmen uttered even the mildest of protests. Others of our freedom-loving authoritarian brethren still enjoy a near-total immunity from harsh rhetoric from their American benefactors, as witness the mumbling incoherence of our reaction to Augusto Pinochet's bloody crackdown in Chile or Chun Doo Hwan's head-breaking in South Korea.

For that matter, God forbid that we should say an evil word about the repeal of the short-lived experiment with freedom of expression in China or the stirrings of a purge in Yugoslavia. To earn our silence, it has not been necessary to be pro-democratic, anti-communist or even pro-capitalist. All you had to do was sign on the anti-Soviet line.

As a former State Department spokesman, I'm well aware that my former colleagues will be able to dredge up a handful of two-liners, dutifully produced for the daily briefings and reflecting our soft-spoken concerns about the "mindless cycle of violence," etc., etc., in some of our client states. But they know how little they mean and how sterile they are when compared with the routine litany of thundering denunciation reserved for the sins of, say, Nicaragua.

Thus, to repeat, it is cause for at least some rejoicing when the president decides to spank publicly a regime he has been at some pains to treat with constructive kindness in the past. "Rather late than never" is an appropriate adage, but now that the kingdom of the blind has a one-eyed king, he ought to look around and select some other targets of opportunity as well.

This may be naive. Perhaps he is only responding to the recent public protests and high-level demonstrations against South Africa, hoping to co-opt and blunt them. But I'd rather believe otherwise, that the president changed his mind on his own, or with a little help from his friends, such as the new chairman of the Senate Foreign Relations Committee, Richard Lugar, or the 35 conservatives in the House who have urged a more vocal opposition to apartheid. If that is the case, he might want to study something one of the 35 wrote in a recent column in the Washington Post. With apologies for heavy editing, part of what Rep. Vin Weber of Minnesota had to say follows:

"Under conservative guidance, America must clearly define the moral basis for its leadership in the world. . . . If conservatives look to freedom as the dominant guiding principle in domestic policies, should we not look for the same in the international arena? . . . But if conservatives are to lead the free world into the 21st century, we must do so on the basis that has a firm and consistent moral foundation. We must stand firmly for freedom and democracy, and that does not permit us to blind our eyes to a government that denies both to the vast majority of its citizens. . . .

"Our policy will have a far greater chance of success if it is part of a comprehensive and consistent support for political and economic freedom wherever it is threatened. . . ."

Jimmy Carter could have said, and indeed did say, virtually the same thing when he was in office. If what is now going on in Washington, from the president to the House conservatives, is the first stirring of a new resolve to put a consistently applied, publicly expressed human-rights policy at the center of American foreign policy, then the second Reagan administration carries hopes that the first one dashed for millions of people around the globe.

Yesterday, Moscow and Pretoria. Tomorrow, Santiago and Seoul?

April 4, 1985

There are no easy answers in South Africa, but the questions are old enough to demand that Washington do a better job of dealing with them. The fundamental issue is clear, as clear as when it was outlined by Martin Luther King 20 years ago:

"In South Africa today, all opposition to white supremacy is condemned as communism, and in its name, due process is destroyed. A medieval segregation is organized with 20th-century efficiency and drive; a sophisticated form of slavery is imposed by a minority upon a majority which is kept in grinding poverty; the dignity of human personality is defiled, and world opinion is arrogantly defied."

Apologists to the contrary, nothing has fundamentally changed in 20 years, though various U.S. governments have tried approaches to Pretoria ranging from today's "constructive engagement" to yesterday's public criticism and clear distancing. None has been marked by urgency. None has had a discernible effect, if effect is to be measured by meaningful change in what is called grand, as opposed to petty, apartheid. No matter how it is viewed, U.S. policy in South Africa has been a failure, particularly if you believe the words of successive presidents who have regularly, if ritualistically, denounced as unacceptable the legally enshrined, totalitarian racism that defines South Africa's bounds.

Today, business as usual is no longer tolerable. Nor are formalistic words of denunciation unaccompanied by anything stronger. It is not enough that President Reagan has finally found it possible to overbalance his words of solicitude for white South African sensibilities with measured condemnation of apartheid. Constructive engagement's only real fruits are growing anti-Americanism among black South Africans and the insolent military interference of South Africa in neighboring countries.

And now the day of escalating violence, so long predicted, seems upon us, and the U.S. must offer more than evenhandedness or hand-wringing. As we contemplate next steps, it is worth noting that the South African government has changed the name of its police ministry from "Justice" to "Law and Order," an Orwellian slip of the bureaucratic brain that says just about everything that needs to be said about justice and the police in that police state.

Police state is the right term. Any country in which less than 20% of the population uses laws, police and army to control the majority is a police state. Any nation that says persons of darker skin or mixed racial ancestry are subject to arbitrary resettlement and systematic denationalization is a police state.

(Denationalization is a subject about which the State Department's human-rights spokesman was correctly, but uncharacteristically, vocal this week as it applied to Bulgaria's treatment of its ethnic Turks.)

South Africa is obviously not the world's only totalitarian society. It is, however, the only one that claims membership in the fraternity of Western democracies. It is that claim which Washington must reject not only in word but by deed.

Nevertheless, the process can and must begin with words. The president of the United States, a nation formed on the proposition of man's political equality, must say without equivocation that we cannot be associated beyond coolly correct links of formal diplomacy with a slave state that invokes the images of Western civilization to mask the policies of Hitler. That alone would do more to undercut the pretentions of Pretoria and its claims to implicit outside acceptance than all the proposals currently before Congress for one form of economic sanction or another.

As for sanctions, however they are defined, two points need to be kept in mind. The first is that in two centuries of using sanctions, the U.S. has never been successful, if "successful" suggests capitulation by the targets. "Red" China, Castro's Cuba, Ian Smith's Rhodesia and the Soviet Union are only the most recent cases.

The second is that it is sometimes necessary to take steps that, whatever their practical effect, have important symbolic meaning. Whether or not the grain embargo and the Olympic boycott had any effect whatsoever on the Soviet Union after its invasion of Afghanistan, it was imperative that Washington say clearly that business-as-usual was impossible. Such should be the consideration when picking and choosing among the options currently being studied on Capitol Hill and resisted by the White House.

A president who routinely denounces the Soviet Union and prods America's allies to restrict their trade with Moscow ought to be able to understand such a recommendation. While he and Secretary of State George Shultz repeatedly claim that the U.S. must be closely engaged with another country if we are to have any leverage, their example in Geneva today, points in another direction. That example ought to be applied immediately to South Africa while there is still a chance to influence the course of events. Otherwise, they will continue to run to the detriment of all South Africans, and America's self-interest as well.

"South Africa needs peace, not violence; dialogue, not confrontation and repression," Secretary Shultz said this week. All true enough, but neither peace nor dialogue is possible without justice—and that's not the same as law and order.

December 10, 1987

A specter seems to be haunting a large number of Americans who are paid to comment on public affairs. It might be called the ghost of *glasnost* future, when a gulled West lays down its arms and takes up its chains. Their commentary has peaked during this remarkable summit week in Washington, but their thinly veiled contempt for the intelligence of most of the rest of us has been just below the surface for a long time. As they see it, the sinisterly effective Soviet propaganda of the Gorbachev era has found a receptive sounding board in the Western public at large.

Forget the predictable fusillades of such "useful idiots" of the radical right as Howard Phillips. They are paid to play Chicken Little and love the role. Mr. Phillips and his mates will say just about anything to command 20 seconds on the national news, and it usually is some variation on "the Russians are coming and the sky is falling."

But far more serious people also profess themselves to be deeply worried. Some suggest that the Gorbachev phenomenon is weakening our awareness that "there can be no moral equality between a democracy and a dictatorship," as A. M. Rosenthal succinctly put it in a New York Times collumn this week. For Mr. Rosenthal, the ephemeral reaction in Europe and America to the seemingly spontaneous Soviet leader could presage an ominous, more permanent shift in public attitudes.

"Skepticism about glasnost is not quite fashionable in the world of political fashion," he wrote. What world is he talking about? What fashion? Certainly not the world reflected in the columns and commentary offered by the newspapers and journals read by most of us, whether in Washington, New York, Chicago, Houston or Miami. Who is awarding "the Soviet dictatorship full moral equality with the U.S.," to pull out another Rosenthal quote? Most of what I read and hear has caution firmly at the center.

Then there are those who think the exponential growth of Soviet spokesmen on American television is preparing the way for the decline of the West. They have been making lists of the amount of air time given to the smooth minions of Moscow. Having done so, they leave the impression that this growth has been matched by American acceptance of the Kremlin line. (The logical implication of their work is that we must be protected from such subversion, an idea that in itself represents the triumph of a familiar Soviet refrain.)

But, as poll after poll demonstrates, they are just plain wrong. Whatever the personal impression that Mikhail Gorbachev is making, and it is quite positive these days, it does not translate into new readiness to accept Soviet policy. No matter how glibly the new men of the Soviet Union emulate American politicians in parrying the thrusts of a Ted Koppel, the public simply hasn't been misled or beguiled. Bemused, yes, at least occasionally, but hoodwinked not at all.

The reason, which should be apparent to those who work in our business and have inherited our political tradition, is that so long as the people have the full range of facts, they can separate wheat from chaff. They have the necessary information about the Soviet invasion of Afghanistan and the Soviet state's long-term invasion of human rights at home—and they oppose both. They have it about the meaning for mankind of an unbridled nuclear arms race, which they would like to see ended.

In other words, they can differentiate—and they do so regularly. They are able to oppose American policy in some sections of the world, such as Nicaragua, while continuing to support the president whose Central American policy they oppose. If that is perplexing to some and frustrating to others, so be it. But it is also considerably more sophisticated than the worries of their detractors.

Let me quickly admit that if you went to too many parties of a certain sort, you could easily believe that all Americans (and by inference, everyone in the West) are silly geese who think that pious references to our shared humanity are the beginning and end of any discussion of world affairs. There is a small but quite visible minority here and abroad that actually believes that sharing a toast is the same as sharing a philosophy, and at times like this, it becomes more visible.

But the America and the Americans I know are far better represented on the streets of Washington this week than in many of the anxious columns. They demonstrate with fervor, look on with interest, weigh options with concern and, at end of day, make up their minds on the basis of a rather extraordinary mix of facts, prejudices, media messages, past perceptions and common sense. They are often wrong in the short run, as are we all, but in the long run their ability to cut through the baloney has been demonstrated repeatedly. If I'm wrong on this, and the worriers are right, we can forget about the machinations of our overseas adversaries. The democratic experiment already is doomed here at home.

DATE	BORROWER'S NAME	